VOSPER THORNYCROFT BUILT WARSHIPS

by Trevor Piper

The Royal Australian Navy Daring Class Destroyer ***HMAS Duchess*** comes alongside the Supply Ship ***HMAS Supply*** in the Great Australian Blight to take on fuel. Originally built for the Royal Navy by Thornycroft at Woolston and launched in 1951, the ship was transferred to Australia in 1964 to replace ***HMAS Voyager*** which was lost in a collision. The ship was converted into a training ship in 1972. *(Ross Gillett)*

Foreword

This book of photographs throws a fascinating light on the origins of VT plc. The company is now, in 2006, a major player in the provision of Government Support Services of all kinds in Britain and abroad, as well as being a shipbuilder. It was not always so.

Shipbuilding is an industry prone to the ups and downs of workload more than most, simply because any new order is as a rule, quite large in relation to its current workload, with the result that it can suffer unwelcome times of feast and famine. When the company was privatised in 1985 it was decided to "broaden the base" to diversify and smooth out these fluctuations. Today with a new and very modem shipyard in Portsmouth, which is thriving, shipbuilding turnover is but a quarter ofVT's total turnover of about £800m.

The photographs, each with a descriptive caption, begin in the 1860's on the Thames at Chiswick where John I Thomycroft started his career as a naval architect. He became a national leader of the profession concentrating on high speed and the fast developing weaponry of small warships. Herbert Vosper began more prosaically as a small boatbuilder in Old Portsmouth, but a chance opportunity after he retired brought in Commander Peter du Cane in 1932 and he it was who pressed ahead with very fast small craft both naval and civilian. In 1904 Thomycroft's had moved to Woolston in Southampton because the London bridges were constraining their activities so the majority of the pictures are of a wide variety of ships, mainly warships, which they built throughout and between two world wars.

Sir David Brown Chairman of Vosper Ltd made a successful bid to take over J I Thomycroft in 1966 giving rise to Vosper Thornycroft Limited and a period of rapid growth until the company was nationalised, after vigorous opposition, in 1977. Eight years later it was privatised by means of a Management Buy Out and was floated on the Stock Exchange in 1988.

As the photographs towards the end of the book show, VT Shipbuilding is now building the fore ends of the Type 45 destroyers and ***HMS Clyde*** for the Royal Navy and achieving high productivity in doing so. It will take an important part in the new aircraft carrier programme and will I expect too, win export work again soon.

Peter Usher
President VT Group

Author's Notes

A rare visit to Lodge Hill in the summer of 2003 to show my face led to a discussion with Steve Bush about a new series of books that Maritime Books were thinking of publishing about British Warship builders. The inevitable question was then asked: how would you like to write one of them. As I work for Vosper Thornycroft I suppose I was an obvious choice. Having never written anything longer than a 4 page magazine article before I reserved my position and said I would look into it and get back to Steve.

On the drive back to Winchester the project seemed more exciting and I decided that I would take it on providing I could gain access to the company photographic archives at Woolston. A phone call to Phil Rood the PR Director the next day gave the green light so I set about reviewing the material available which turned out to be extensive as far as Thornycroft's were concerned, but quite light in the early days of Vosper's. Armed with this I confirmed to Steve that the project was feasible so I embarked on research and photograph collection. Unfortunately at this time the Woolston Shipyard was being run down and moved to Portsmouth Naval Base, and this included the photographic archives so I had to quickly select a suitable cross section of photographs from across both companies that were interesting and showed the Companies products over the 150 years since JI Thornycroft built his first vessel. For those of you who have never done this it is a daunting task as many were unmarked and not dated. My thanks must go at this point to Julian Hickman the Company Photographer for his patience and help. Selecting the photographs was actually easy compared with researching and writing the captions. This took me the best part of 2 years to complete and many hours reading or at the computer.

In the pages following I hope that you will find a completed pictorial history of two quite different shipbuilders who came together in 1966 to form the nucleus of what is probably the most successful current UK shipbuilder. My thanks go to the VT Group for the majority of the photographs, Paul Sallabank for his advice, Julian Hickman, David Briggs for the loan of his father's records and photographs, Ross Gillett for his Australian input and the Maritime Photo Library for the rare view of ***HMS Latona***.

Trevor Piper
2006

First published in the United Kingdom in 2006 by Maritime Books, Lodge Hill, Liskeard, Cornwall, PL14 4EL

Vosper Thornycroft Built Warships

This well established Company, known for the high quality of their products, was formed in 1966 with the joining of two very different shipbuilding companies, Vosper Ltd of Portsmouth, famous for high speed craft and motor torpedo boats, and JI Thornycroft of Southampton, mainly noted for Destroyer building. The merged Company survived the trauma of being nationalised by the Labour Government in the mid 1970's when it became a division of British Shipbuilders, and returned to the commercial sector with a management buyout in late 1985. The Company has never looked back since privatisation and has continued to flourish during the lean periods of warship building, mainly through intensive and successful sales efforts for export and diversification outside of its core shipbuilding business into the training and support areas.

Herbert Edward Vosper set up his Company, Vosper & Co when he was only 21 in 1871 at Camber, a small commercial dock on the east side of the entrance to Portsmouth harbour. The main work of the Company during the early years was largely in the refitting and repair of coastal vessels. The soon prosperous company began producing their own range of steam reciprocating engines which were fitted into all types of craft, including yachts, tugs, tenders and launches, for the Admiralty and for export. One of the first vessels that the Company built was the tug ***Hercules*** for the Shoreham Harbour Authority. Vosper & Co. proved to be an early pioneer of the internal combustion engine, developing vaporising paraffin and crude oil engines.

In the early days, the Company was not known as a builder of high speed craft, but mainly for the reliability and strength of their products. It had a wide range of skills and capacities, being able to design, develop and build its own hulls in steel and in wood, engines, boilers and associated machinery, in fact the whole ship. Well into the 20th Century, they were still listed as Engineers and Boiler makers. The Great War saw a rapid expansion of the company's activities, but with the cessation of hostilities in late 1918 Vosper existed mainly on refit work. A major contract at that time was the virtual rebuild of Captain Scott's ***Discovery*** for a further Antarctic expedition. Herbert Vosper retired in 1919, and died in 1934.

Vosper & Co's fortunes changed when Commander Du Cane became managing director in 1931. The Company then concentrated on high speed craft, including yachts, tenders and racing boats. Sir Malcolm Campbell's ***Bluebird II*** was built by the company and took the world water speed record at 141.7mph in August 1939. In 1936, Vosper & Co. became a public company and changed its name to Vosper Ltd, and a second yard was purchased at Flathouse on the north side of Portsmouth Dockyard. This yard was later compulsorily purchased by the Admiralty and a new site established at Portchester which is still in use today. Commander Du Cane built as a private venture a 68ft motor torpedo boat, which achieved 48 knots on trials. The Admiralty then purchased this boat and commissioned it as ***MTB102***. The boat still survives today in working order preserved in the Norwich area. ***MTB102*** was the prototype for a further 350 boats built at home and abroad by Vosper's during WWII and gained the Company a deserved reputation as a provider of well built and reliable fast attack craft. In 1939 came a novel order from the Admiralty to build and deliver a new barge for the Royal Yacht ***Victoria & Albert***. In 1938 Vosper began to develop a new generation of motor torpedo boats, which laid the foundations for the company's later concentration on small high speed warships, mainly using the un-stepped planning hull design. To power these boats, Vosper obtained a licence to manufacture the Italian Isotta Franschini engine, later developed to produce nearly 1500hp. When the supply of these engines became difficult due to the war, Packard engines were fitted. At the end of the war, Vosper had amassed a great deal of expertise and experience relating to all aspects of high speed craft, the only problem was how to apply this experience to a deflated post war market.

The 73ft MTB1601 was built in 1948, and incorporated a number of novel Vosper ideas including a modified hull form with a higher chine and deeper V section hull, and controllable pitch propellers with direct drive. The vessel originally had no gearboxes, but was later refitted with fixed pitch propellers and reversing gearboxes on which she achieved 43knots on trials. This hull design became the basis for later Vosper designs including the Brave Class fast patrol boats. Vospers were then selected to pioneer the installation of marine gas turbines with the fitting of a Rolls Royce RM60 into the former steam gunboat ***HMS Grey Goose***. This installation was swiftly followed by the building of the two Bold Class vessels fitted with Metro-Vickers G2 gas turbines. Despite this work, there was not the volume or profit to sustain the company, and there is no doubt that without the intervention of the Korean War which led to an emergency construction programme of fast patrol boats, Vosper Ltd as a company would probably have ceased trading.

The 1950's saw the building of the Brave Class powered by the Bristol Siddeley Proteus gas turbine using super cavitating propellers developed in the Vosper's cavitation tunnel at Portchester. Later developments of this design led to speeds of up to 58 knots being achievable. In 1958, the controlling shares in Vosper Ltd were purchased by the Mineral Separation Company which provided the financial support needed to sustain the Company into the 1960's, during which time a number of larger twin and triple screw fast patrols boats were built for the German, Danish, Malaysian, Brunei and Libyan Navies. The Company also designed and built even larger corvettes and fast patrol boats for Ghana, Peru, and Singapore, four of which came from the Singapore shipyard. This was a profitable time for the company, and in 1963 the controlling interest was purchased by the David Brown Corporation. In 1965, the Vosper design team in collaboration with Vickers, completed the design of its first frigate known as the Mk 5. This ship would displace 1300 tons and be capable of 40 knots, however the ship could not be built at any of the current Vosper facilities, but in the event the strong financial position of the Company allowed a merger with JI Thornycroft of Southampton. This merger provided the larger building capacity required for Vosper's to expand.

JI Thornycroft built his first vessel at Chiswick on the River Thames in the late 1800's, and was a pioneer in the production of high speed vessels. Thornycroft specialised in the development of fast steam powered torpedo boats and destroyers achieving speeds that were previously considered unobtainable by many leading architects. The main JI Thornycroft shipyard was established on the side of the River Itchen at Woolston Southampton and continued to serve the company well until the new modular shipbuilding facility in Portsmouth Dockyard was constructed in 2003. The Woolston shipyard was always one of Southampton's major employers, and delivered its first ship to the Royal Navy, ***HMS Tartar*** in 1906. The yard had several slips, but the width of the River Itchen limited the length of the ship built to that of a large destroyer. In the period up to the start of the Great War, Thornycroft's built 37 destroyers for the RN alone, and several more for export.

There has always been a saying in the Royal Navy that if you were serving on a Thornycroft built ship then you were serving on a well built and sound vessel. Many a famous ship has been built at Woolston, and they proved to be well able to take serious damage and still survive to fight another day. During the First World War, Thornycroft built 26 destroyers, 3 submarines, and a huge number of coastal motor boats and fast launches all powered by petrol engines and able to carry torpedoes.

After the Great War, despite the dramatic rundown in the size of the Royal Navy, the company survived and continued to build destroyer sized warships both for the Admiralty and for export, and benefitted from the large shipbuilding programmes of the late 1930's as Britain once again geared up for war. The Woolston shipyard was bombed and damaged several times during the Blitz, probably because the Supermarine Spitfire factory was the next industrial facility upriver and Southampton was a major port. Certainly, the air raids became less frequent when the Spitfire factory was burnt out and aircraft production transferred to outlying sites. Thornycroft built a huge and diverse number of ships during the war from minelayers, destroyers and corvettes, to landing craft and RAF rescue launches. The company also designed and built the improved Hunt Class destroyers ***Bissenden*** and ***Brecon*** which corrected the stability problems experienced by the original design.

Once again with the run down of the Royal Navy after 1945, Thornycroft reverted to what can only be called lean production, with work being confined to building tugs, ferries, launches and barges, with the occasional naval order to be completed. The company launched the Weapons Class destroyer ***Crossbow*** in 1946, and the Daring Class destroyer ***Duchess*** in 1951. The Korean War provided a respite, with the building of 10 Ton class wooden minesweepers and three frigates. The Type 12 frigate ***HMNZS Otago*** was delivered in 1960, by which time naval orders were once again scarce. One of the problems which Thornycroft experienced at this time was the lack of weapons expertise within the company, all weapons dealings were with Vickers, who were also competing in the same market for falling orders, and who naturally would promote their own shipbuilding division. The Tribal Class general purpose frigate ***Gurkha*** was delivered to the RN in 1963 and the Leander Class frigate ***Juno*** laid down in 1964. The minelayer ***Abdiel*** followed in 1965 along with two 78ft patrol boats for Kuwait. These were lean times for the company, but the Board wisely invested in the future of the company by continually improving the Woolston facility with the extension on the quays and other facilities, and closed the loss making yard on the Thames.

The company also instigated what was to be a far sighted study into the feasibility of producing a Glass Reinforced Plastic (GRP) hull. Although the company had a huge range of capabilities and engineering skills, its profit margins were low, and it was open to a hostile take over, so the approach from Vosper to merge the two companies' gave them both a lifeline and outlets to succeed. In early 1966 they joined forces, but both companies continued to trade under their original names until June 1970 when the title Vosper Thornycroft (VT) was adopted. The new expanded company became very vigorous in the export market, with salesmen travelling the world to secure shipbuilding contracts for the company. Orders were realised for a corvette and a support ship for Libya, three fast patrol craft for Kenya, and a large order of 18 patrol craft for Malaysia. VT were also very successful in selling warships to the Shah of Iran, beginning with the refitting and updating of the ex RN Battle Class destroyer ***HMS Sluys*** to be renamed ***Artemiz***. This work was followed by the order of 4 Mark 5 frigates, two of which were built by Vickers to share the financial and construction risk. These innovative heavily armed steel ships employed a CODAG propulsion system with Rolls-Royce Olympus gas turbines capable of driving the vessels at 40 knots using super cavitating propellers. This order was followed early in 1968 with a slightly larger Mk 7 Frigate for Libya. In 1967, a design for the replacement of the successful Leander Class was urgently required, but resource problems within the MoD meant that the ship could not be designed in-house, so VT in partnership with Yarrows on the Clyde submitted a proposal for a 3000 ton Frigate that was to become the Type 21. The joint bid was successful, and the Woolston shipyard built the first of class ***Amazon***. The hull was built of steel and the superstructure of aluminium; this was later to cause controversy when ***Antelope*** and ***Ardent*** were lost in the Falklands war. ***HMS Amazon*** had the distinction of being the first class of ship to go to sea with the now ubiquitous RR Tyne and Olympus machinery combination. This was an innovative power plant at the time, and had in fact been scheduled to first go to sea in the Type 42 Destroyer ***Sheffield***, but the Vickers ship was late in delivery. A further two Type 21's were built at Woolston, ***Antelope*** and **Active**, with the remaining five built at Yarrows. In early 1970, the Brazilian Navy issued a requirement for up to six new Frigates, and the VT design, the Mk 10 was based on an enlarged Type 21. The bid was accepted and the contract signed in September 1970. Four would be built at Woolston and two in Brazil with assistance and technology transfer from VT. A new covered shipbuilding facility was built at Woolston to help complete this prestigious order.

The Portchester yard was also busy at this time, delivering two 110ft steel patrol boats to Singapore, with another two of the class being built at the Company's Singapore yard. The Royal Navy received the fast training boats ***Scimitar***, ***Cutlass*** and ***Sabre***, and Nigeria had two Mk 3 Frigates. Also in 1970, two 103ft patrol boats were built for Panama and two more went to Trinidad.

In 1974, the newly elected Labour government introduced a bill to nationalise the shipbuilding industry. After a long hard fought battle against the bill, mainly from the warship builders, the Company was nationalised on 1 July 1977, and became a division of British Shipbuilders. Aside from the bureaucratic interference, many people felt that VT in the prosperous south would be sacrificed for those shipbuilding concerns in the north of the country. Luckily this fear proved unfounded. VT did however secure an early export order from Egypt for six 52m Ramadan class patrol boats. The Woolston yard received orders for three Type 42 Destroyers, ***Southampton***, ***Nottingham*** and ***Gloucester***, the later proving to be the last large steel ship to be built at Woolston until the Trimaran ***Triton*** was launched in 2000. In 1982, the production of the Hunt Class GRP Minehunters was in full swing, with eleven of the class of thirteen constructed by VT.

The Woolston shipyard was heavily tasked during the Falklands crisis in the conversion of the Liners ***Canberra*** and ***QE2*** into troopships. This work mainly involved the fitting of helicopter decks and refuelling at sea equipment, and required working in substantial reinforcing steelwork to support the heavy helicopter decks high up on the liner's aluminium superstructures. This work was accomplished in record time, reflecting the pride, experience and expertise available in the Company. Vosper Thornycroft were also asked by the MoD to undertake a study into what form the next generation of Minehunter should take. This ship eventually materialised into the Single Role Minehunter (SRMH) Sandown Class. VT also secured some welcome steel ship work at this time with the refit of three ex RN Tribal Class frigates for Indonesia.

The first SRMH, ***Sandown*** was handed over in 1989, and in addition to the other RN ships, VT also built three more for Saudi Arabia under the enormous BAE Systems Al Yamamah contract. At least the GRP facility was busy, but major steel ship work still eluded the Company despite extensive sales efforts. By 1992 work was again scarce, and a further 350 redundancies were declared. Later that year however the sales team had success with the sale of two 83m corvettes for the Government of Oman. This was immediately followed by an order for four 56m strike craft for the State of Qatar, and in 1994, the RN ordered a second batch of seven SRMH. After several years of promoting innovative warship designs, including the revolutionary ***Sea Wraith*** stealth ship, VT were awarded a contract to build the Trimaran demonstrator ***RV Triton***. This advanced ship was launched in May 2000. Modular construction techniques enabled Triton to be launched almost 97% complete. In late 1999, VT secured a major export order against strong opposition to design and support the construction of a number of 62m Super Vita fast attack craft for Greece at the Elefis Shipyard near Athens for the Hellenic Navy. As part of this innovative contract, VT transferred shipbuilding technology and supplied two ex Royal Navy Hunt Class Minehunters

In Early 2000, the Company was selected as prime contractor for a £100m order to supply two new survey vessels for the RN, to be named ***Enterprise*** and ***Echo***. Capacity issues at the Woolston yard led to build of these two ships being sub-contracted to the Appeldore Shipyard in Devon. In a completely innovative move, VT formulated an unsolicited bid to the UK Government to replace the five Island Class OPV's with three new leased River Class vessels that would be guaranteed available to the RN for up to 300 days per year. The package includes whole life support, and the option for the RN to purchase the vessels at the end of the 5 year lease or return the vessels to VT. The last of these three ships, ***Mersey*** launched on 25 June 2003, turned out to be the final steel ship to be constructed by the Company at Woolston.

The prospect of major large steel ship work retuned to the Company when it was announced in July 2000 that VT was to share in the construction programme of the new Type 45 Destroyers for the RN. After careful consideration of the continued viability of the Woolston shipyard, it was decided to move the shipbuilding facility from Woolston to a new purpose built shipyard in Portsmouth Dockyard the land for which was secured on a 125 year lease. This yard is one of the most modern shipbuilding facilities in the world, and the first steel was cut for ***Daring*** in late October 2003. The construction of this new shipbuilding facility proved to be doubly important, as in early 2003, the Government announced that VT will share in building mega-blocks for the two new Aircraft Carriers ***HMS Queen Elizabeth*** and ***HMS Prince of Wales.*** In 2005, VT presented the MoD with an unsolicited bid similar to that which produced the River Class to replace the two Castle Class offshore patrol Vessels with a single ship, based on a helicopter capable River Class vessel. The bid was successful, and the resulting ship, designated an OPV(H), ***Clyde*** was laid down in the shipbuilding facility at Portsmouth in June 2005 and is due for delivery to the RN in September 2006. She will be the first whole warship built at Portsmouth dockyard for four decades. To add to this success, it was announced in May 2006 that VT had been selected as the preferred bidder to supply the Oman Navy with three advanced OPV's all to be built at Portsmouth. These substantial contracts will ensure that warship building will continue on the south coast until at least the year 2020.

Mr John Issac Thornycroft with his first steam powered vessel ***Nautilus*** at Chiswick on the River Thames in 1862. He was only 16 years old when he started the boat's construction in 1859 after making various model engines, and the 36ft long steam launch was fitted with a twin cylinder reciprocating engine and a railway locomotive type boiler. It was the first steam launch that proved capable of keeping pace with the 'eights' in the University Boat Race. Flushed with this success, his father purchased the land at Chiswick and the firm of JI Thornycroft was founded there in 1864. *(VT Group)*

The Admiralty purchased the patent rights to the Whitehead torpedo in 1871 for £15,000, and the availability of this weapon allowed them to order a suitable vessel to deploy it. ***HMS Lightning*** was the first Torpedo Boat delivered by the company to the Royal Navy and was the pioneer in the field of small naval torpedo carrying craft. Designed and built at Chiswick in 1876, the 81 ft long vessel was powered by a two cylinder compound steam engine which developed 390hp at 450rpm to achieve 18.5 knots. The torpedo was launched from a tube fitted over the forward deck. *(VT Group)*

An early view of the Woolston shipyard site on the east side of the River Itchen in 1880 looking across towards Southampton Docks. John I Thornycroft transferred his main shipbuilding yard here from Church Wharf at Chiswick on the River Thames because the increasing size of the ships being constructed by the company was being severely limited by the capacity available at Chiswick and the need to lower the ships superstructure to clear the Thames bridges. *(VT Group)*

The launch of a Royal Navy ship at Chiswick on the River Thames was always a social occasion, although somewhat dangerous for the viewing public in the small boats on the opposite Surrey bank. The Torpedo Gun Boat ***HMS Speedy*** is launched in the summer of 1893. The 242ft long ship introduced the new 3 drum boiler into RN service and her 4705shp triple expansion engines could drive the ship at 20 knots. *(VT Group)*

Shipyard managers at Chiswick find time to pose for the camera on launch day in the summer of 1893 of the Torpedo Gun Boat ***HMS Speedy***, the only Torpedo Gun Boat built at Chiswick. The ram bow, always a feature of early British warships is shown to good effect. The ship proved to be a good seaboat, and rendered useful service on foreign commissions, but her slow speed led to the development of an entirely new class, the Torpedo Boat Destroyer. *(VT Group)*

HMS Daring was an A Class 'Turtle Back' Destroyer that was delivered by Thornycroft's at Chiswick in 1893. She was one of six similar ships of the class that had torpedo tubes on the bow in addition to those on deck, but with this arrangement the ship tended to over-run the torpedoes when fired ahead. The triple expansion engines could drive the 180 ft long ship at over 28 knots, and for the first time the phenomenon now known as propeller cavitation was experienced. ***HMS Daring*** was sold for scrapping in 1912. *(VT Group)*

The River Gunboat ***HMS Melik*** was completed by Thornycroft's at Chiswick in 1896 for service in Egypt. She was one of three similar ships the design of which was based on the River Nile steamers built for the relief of Khartoum, but with more power and bullet protection. ***HMS Melik*** played a part in the Omburman campaign and was eventually retired to become the floating clubhouse for the Khartoum Yacht Club. She survives to this day. *(VT Group)*

HMS Albatross was a C Class 'Turtle Back' Destroyer that was built by Thornycroft's at Chiswick and completed in 1898. She was one of 60 similar ships delivered to the Royal Navy between 1895 and 1902, although the ship had increased length and more power. Her triple expansion engines developed 7,600shp and the twin screws drove the ship at 31knots, which was slated as the highest speed that could be obtained using reciprocating machinery. ***HMS Albatross*** survived the Great War and was sold for scrapping in 1920. *(VT Group)*

The 30 knot Torpedo Boat Destroyer ***HMS Cygnet*** is prepared for launching at the Chiswick shipyard at the close of the 19th century with the majority of the securing chocks removed. The vessel is dressed overall and will be launched without propellers to avoid damage in the relatively shallow waters of the River Thames. The 210ft long twin screw ship was powered by triple expansion engines which developed 5,500 shp and was one of four similar ships ordered from Thornycroft's at the same time. The well dressed launching party can be seen beside the ship prior to the actual launch ceremony. *(VT Group)*

Thornycroft were early pioneers of the internal combustion engine, developing crude oil semi-diesel engines. The photograph shows an early 1900's 200hp four cylinder compression ignition engine with fresh water injection for piston cooling. *(VT Group)*

One of the last ships built for the Royal Navy at Chiswick, the 'Turtle Back' destroyer ***HMS Gladfly*** is shown running sea trials off the Spithead Forts in 1906. One of six similar ships constructed by Thornycroft's, the class introduced two important innovations to destroyer design with the introduction of turbine machinery and oil fired boilers. The triple screw168ft long vessel developed 5,500 shp and was capable of just over 27 knots. She was renamed ***TB6*** soon after commissioning. *(VT Group)*

The four funnelled F (Tribal) Class Destroyer ***HMS Tartar*** was the first Royal Navy ship launched at the new Woolston shipyard in 1907. The triple screw steam turbine powered vessel made 37.4knots on trials making her the fastest ship of her day. The short funnels were lengthened in 1911 as the corrosive boiler uptake gases often made occupation of the bridge untenable. ***HMS Tartar*** survived the Great War and was sold shortly after for scrapping in 1921. *(VT Group)*

The Tribal Class destroyer ***HMS Amazon*** was virtually a repeat of the earlier ***HMS Tartar***, and was delivered from Thornycroft's Woolston shipyard in 1908. The triple screw steam turbine powered vessel was capable of 35 knots and she was armed with five 12 pdr guns and twin 18-inch torpedo tubes. Along with her Woolston built twin sister ***HMS Nubian***, the ***Amazon*** spent most of her war on the Dover patrol, and was sold for scrapping soon after the wars ending in 1919. *(VT Group)*

Vosper built a number of 50ft Coastal Motor Boats with a stepped hull form during the first World War. One is shown at speed in the Solent. The hull design was developed from the successful racing hydroplane ***Miranda IV*** built at Vosper's Broad street Yard in Old Portsmouth in 1910. Speed was in excess of 30 knots and they were powered by a variety of engines, mainly American, although a number were fitted with Thornycroft engines. The torpedoes were launched from the stern. *(VT Group)*

The newly completed L Class Destroyer ***HMS Lance*** in the Solent in early 1914. She was one of two 3 funneled L Class Destroyers completed by Thornycroft's at Woolston. The steam turbine powered vessel was capable of 31 knots and was armed with three 4-inch guns and four 21-inch torpedo tubes. ***HMS Lance*** was running trials at Maplin in early August 1914 when she was recalled by the Admiralty and ordered to commission at once and join the Harwich Destroyer force. She fired the first shot of the war in anger at the German ship ***Koningen Luise*** which was caught laying mines in the Thames estuary on 5 August. Although only five years old, she had a hard war and was sold for scrapping in 1921.
(VT Group)

The launch of the Admiralty M Class destroyer ***HMS Michael*** at Woolston in 1915. One of the early straight stemmed vessels with short funnels, she was one of six M Class ships built by Thornycroft. Armed with three 4-inch guns in single gun mounts, and four 21-inch torpedo tubes, the steam turbine powered ship was capable of 34 knots. She was credited with sinking a U-Boat in 1918. ***HMS Michael*** survived the war and was sold for scrapping in 1921. *(VT Group)*

The Submarine ***E33*** was launched at Woolston in April 1915 and commissioned in November 1916, joining the 9th Flotilla at Harwich for patrols in the North Sea. On 2 December 1918 she collided with a tug towing the surrendered ***U-155***, but escaped undamaged. In November 1919 ***E33*** was detailed for Oceanographic duties before reducing to the reserve in June 1921. She was sold for scrap at Cashmore, Newport in September 1922. *(VT Group)*

The three funneled ***HMS Mastiff*** was one of six Thornycroft M Type Destroyers built at Woolston between 1914-1916. ***HMS Mastiff*** was modified by Thornycroft's to have increased speed as it was believed that the latest German ships were faster than the standard Admiralty design. She was also slightly heavier at 1,070 tons, but the steam turbines could drive the ship at 37 knots. Shown newly completed in Southampton Water, ***HMS Mastiff*** survived the war and was sold for scrapping in 1921.

(VT Group)

The Submarine ***F3*** was one of only three submarines ever built by Thornycroft's at Woolston. Designed by Vickers, she had a partial double hull construction and joined the 8th Submarine flotilla at Great Yarmouth for North Sea patrols. She became a training boat at Portsmouth in September 1917 and was finally paid off at Campbeltown, Kintyre in December 1918. She was sold for scrapping in 1920. *(VT Group)*

The Submarine ***E34*** just before launching on 27 January 1917. The boat was one of the first in the Royal Navy to be fitted as a mine-layer, and the vertical mine tubes through the saddle tanks added to the constructional difficulties. She joined the 9th Flotilla at Harwich on completion and torpedoed and sank ***UB-16*** in the North Sea on 10 May 1918. On 14 July she left Harwich to lay mines off Vlieland, but was never heard of again and was reported lost on 19 July, probably in an uncharted minefield off the Heligoland Blight.
(VT Group)

The three funneled Thornycroft R Type Destroyer ***HMS Teazer*** was completed at Woolston in 1917. One of 5 similar ships built by the Company, the Thornycroft ships had increased shaft horsepower, and the geared turbines made them capable of nearly 40 knots. On trials in 1917, ***HMS Teazer*** achieved just over 40 knots which was a world record speed for Destroyers at the time. Laid up after the Great War for a number of years, she was eventually sold for scrapping in 1931. *(VT Group)*

HMS Shakespeare was one of 3 Thornycroft Flotilla Leaders built at Woolston between 1917 and 1919. Constructed at the request of Admiral Jellicoe who was concerned that the Light Cruisers of the day could not keep up with the destroyers, the 329 ft long steam turbine powered ship displaced 1750 tons and was armed with five 4.7-inch guns in single mounts, one 3-inch anti-aircraft gun and six 21-inch torpedo tubes. Late in the war, she was badly damaged by a mine, with the stern reportedly only attached by the propeller shafts, and had to be towed back to Harwich for major repairs. She was eventually sold for scrapping in 1936. *(VT Group)*

The Thornycroft S Type Destroyer ***HMS Speedy*** was one of five similar ships completed at Woolston in 1918. Developed from the standard Admiralty S Type design the Thornycroft ships developed more power and they all reached over 38 knots on trials. ***HMS Speedy*** foundered in the Sea of Marmora after a collision in 1922.

(VT Group)

Being Southampton based, Thornycroft's were often called upon to overhaul the ocean liners that used the port. This view shows the stern tube of the Cunard liner ***RMS Mauretania*** being rebored on the centre lathe in the Woolston machine shop soon after the ending of World War One. *(David Briggs)*

A view of one end of the general engineering machine shop at Woolston in the inter-war years showing the machinery still driven by the overhead belt drives.
(David Briggs)

Using the overhead crane, boiler makers manoeuvre the bare bones of an Admiralty three drum boiler destined for the D class destroyer ***HMS Decoy*** in the Woolston Boiler shop early in January 1932. The boilers were the first closed feed boilers built at Woolston and had a working pressure of 300 psi and a superheat of 620 degrees. The three drums and riveted boiler endplate can be clearly seen. The ship was launched in June, just five months later. The Woolston works was capable of the manufacture of the majority of a warships machinery, including the turbines and auxiliary machinery. *(David Briggs)*

A general view of the turbine erecting shop at Woolston during the inter-war years. Thornycroft nearly always manufactured the steam machinery for the ships built at Woolston and produced machinery sets for other shipyards that did not have this manufacturing capability.

(David Briggs)

With his supervisor looking on, a worker bends a resin filled copper pipe destined for a warship engine room using a large hydraulic press in the Woolston pipe shop during the inter-war period. One can only imagine what current Health and Safety legislation would make of the lack of guards on the machinery and the worker leaning across the job! *(David Briggs)*

The Canadian Destroyer ***HMCS Saguenay*** in May 1936. She and her sister ship Skeena, which was lost off Iceland in October 1944 were completed at Woolston in 1930. The 1350 ton ships were virtually identical to the Royal Navy A Class and carried five 4.7-inch guns in single turrets. To meet the exacting Canadian conditions, the bows and forward plating were strengthened against ice and the metacentric height was raised as it was estimated that there may be up to 50 or 60 tons of ice on deck in Arctic waters. After a hard war in which she suffered extensive battle and weather damage, ***HMCS Saguenay*** was placed on the disposal list in late 1945. *(VT Group)*

The G Class destroyer ***HMS Glowworm*** and her sister ship ***HMS Grafton*** were launched at Woolston in 1935. The ship introduced the quintruple torpedo tubes into Royal Navy service, and the 34,000shp Parsons geared turbines gave a speed of 35 knots. Both ships had short service lives, ***Grafton*** was lost at Dunkirk, and ***Glowworm*** was sunk off Norway on the 8th of April 1940 by gunfire from the German Heavy Cruiser ***Admiral Hipper*** after the destroyer had rammed the German ship. Her Captain, Lt Cdr GB Roope was awarded the Victoria Cross for the action. *(VT Group)*

The Tribal Class Destroyer ***HMS Mohawk*** running trials in Southampton Water. Launched at Woolston in October 1937 she was one of a Class of 16 ordered under the 1935/36 naval estimates, of which only four survived WWII. The Class showed a notable increase in size and power over the preceding G, H, and I Classes and they were heavily armed with eight 4.7-inch guns in twin mounts. ***HMS Mohawk*** was lost off Cap Bon in the Mediterranean after she was torpedoed by the Italian destroyer ***Tarigo*** on 16 April 1941, and had to be finally sunk by the Destroyer ***HMS Janus***. *(VT Group)*

In 1937, Vosper's built a private venture prototype 68ft Motor Torpedo Boat with a hard chine hull and no step. The trials in the English Channel in a Force 7 gale convinced a sceptical Admiralty that the Vosper hull form would give them the speed and seaworthiness that they required. The vessel was later renamed ***MTB 102***. The craft was powered by three Isotta Franschini 1000hp petrol engines and attained 48 knots on trials before any armament was fitted. Completely restored, ***MTB 102*** still survives to this day.
(VT Group)

A pre-war photograph of ***MTB 102*** now armed with two 22-inch torpedo tubes in company with an unarmed ***MTB 100*** off the Spithead Forts. ***MTB 102*** was constructed of double diagonal mahogany planking on sawn frames, which was usual in this type of craft until synthetic resin glues and marine plywood were perfected and became available for marine use. *(VT Group)*

The 60ft Vosper built Swedish Motor Torpedo Boat ***T3*** under going sea trials in the Solent in 1939. Delivered just before the start of WWII, the twin 18-inch torpedo tubes were fitted in the UK, but the main gun armament was completed once the vessel reached Sweden. The twin screw vessel was powered by twin Isotta Fraschini petrol engines for high speed and attained 42 knots on trials. Twin Thornycroft V8's were fitted as cruising engines. *(VT Group)*

An early 1939 view of the Swedish MTB ***T3*** fitting out at the Vosper's Broad Street yard in Old Portsmouth. The twin 18-inch torpedo tubes are now in place, but the gun tubs are empty as remaining gun armament will be fitted when the vessel is delivered to Sweden later in the summer. The quality of the Vosper workmanship can clearly be seen in the engine room ventilation uptakes. *(VT Group)*

The 70ft ***MTB 220*** was delivered by Vosper's from the Old Portsmouth yard under the 1940 emergency building programme. Powered by three Packard V12 petrol engines and twin Vosper V8's for cruising the main engines could drive the vessel at 39 knots. The design retained the scalloped sheerline ahead of the torpedo tubes, and the ship was armed with the standard twin 21-inch torpedo tubes, depth charges, and a twin 0.5-inch machine gun turret. *(VT Group)*

Still flying her builders flag and carrying a bowler hatted company representative, ***MTB 35*** carries out pre-delivery trials in Southampton Water in April 1941. She was one of a large number of 71ft MTB's built by Vosper's under the 1939/40 emergency building programme, and was powered by three Scott Hall and one Vosper V8 to give a service speed of 28 knots. The vessel spent the majority of her short service life in the English Channel before being paid off for disposal in November 1943.

(VT Group)

A Vosper's built 40ft MTB constructed for Greece but taken over by the RN on the outbreak of WWII in the upper reaches of Portsmouth Dockyard close to what is now known as Fountain Lake jetty. The vessel is powered by Isotta Fraschini engines. An Admiralty Floating Dry-Dock is shown in the background and the Gunnery School at Whale Island is in the distance. *(VT Group)*

The K class Destroyer ***HMS Kashmir*** and her sister ***Kimberley*** were both launched at Thornycroft's at Woolston within 2 months of each other in the summer of 1939. The K Class were the first longitudinally framed destroyers and the first with only 2 boilers and one funnel built for the Royal Navy and served mostly in the Mediterranean. ***HMS Kimberley*** survived the war and was scrapped at Troon in 1949, but ***Kashmir*** was bombed by German JU87 Stuka dive bombers and sank within two minutes south of Crete on 23 May 1941. *(MoD/Crown Copyright)*

The 70ft ***MTB 347*** on the building slip at Vosper's Broad Street yard in Old Portsmouth in early 1941. The vessel was ordered under an extension to the 1939 building programme and was powered by three Packard V12 and two Vosper V8 petrol engines to give a speed of 39 knots. The standard MTB armament of twin 21-inch torpedo tubes, depth charges and a twin 0.5-inch machine gun turret was fitted. ***MTB 347*** was lost in company with her sister ship ***MTB 360*** on the night of 30 September 1944 whilst attacking a German convoy off the Dutch coast. *(VT Group)*

In 1941 Vospers were asked to develop a new type of air-sea rescue launch with a little less emphasis on speed but more on sea-keeping ability to operate in the region of Lands End to Milford Haven. This design became the 73ft RAF air sea rescue launch of 1941/42 which was based on a scaled down version of the Admiralty Fairmile D design. The newly completed RAF Crash Tender ***2564*** is shown under-going initial sea trials in Southampton Water in early 1942. *(VT Group)*

The newly launched RAF Crash Tender ***2575*** fitting out in late 1941. The vessel is riding high in the water as she has yet to have her engines, armament and other major equipment fitted. The machinery consisted of twin Thornycroft V12 petrol engines for high speed and twin Vosper V8's for cruising, all driving through special flexible couplings and reduction gearing. This installation was the fore- runner of the combined power plants used later with the advent of gas turbines. The vessels were capable of 25 knots.
(VT Group)

The newly completed RAF Crash Tender ***2576*** alongside at Vosper's yard prior to delivery to the RAF in early 1942. The wooden hull construction of double skinned diagonally laid mahogany planks can be clearly seen as the sun shines on the hull in this photograph.The hull chine was higher at the bow and the forefoot fine in section with a large deadrise angle. The bows were flared to give a full deck line. The main armament of three twin 0.5-inch machine gun turrets can be clearly seen. *(VT Group)*

The fast Minelayer ***HMS Latona*** was launched by Thornycroft's at Woolston in August 1940 and commissioned on the 4 May 1941. The 418ft long ship remains the largest warship ever built by the company. Her 72,000shp geared turbines could drive the ship at 40 knots. The ship was armed with six 4-inch guns in twin turrets and could carry 160 mines. Her first task after completion was to carry a consignment of Oerlikon guns and other urgent stores to Alexandria. When barely 6 months old, on the 25 October 1941 whilst carrying a contingent of Australian troops from Tobruk she was bombed and sunk by German dive bombers off Libya.

(Maritime Photo Library)

A view of the southern end of Thornycroft's Woolston shipyard on the River Itchen in late 1941 with five of the fifteen 73-ft RAF air-sea rescue launches in varying stages of fitting out with their Thornycroft V12 engines. Although it would be another 25 years before Vosper and Thornycroft would join forces and amalgamate the volume production of small warfighting craft forced the two companies to work closely together. *(VT Group)*

The Vosper built ***MTB 74*** shown at speed on trials in the Solent with the special foredeck torpedo tube launchers installed for the raid on the great dry-dock at St Nazaire. She was part of the 1940 MTB programme, and was powered by three Packard V12 and two Vosper V8 engines capable of driving the ship at 39 knots. The vessel was armed with two 2-inch torpedo tubes, depth charges and a twin 0.5-inch machine gun. She was lost during the raid whilst stopping to assist another damaged craft, and her crew taken prisoner. *(VT Group)*

The O Class Destroyer ***HMS Opportune*** was launched by Thornycroft's at Woolston in January 1942. The ship had a very active war, taking part in the North African landings, the battle of the North Cape against the German Battlecruiser Scharnhorst, Atlantic convoy duties and was present at the D-Day landings. The O Class were basically simplified versions of the earlier J, K and N Class ships but had 11ft less length and a smaller beam. It is doubtful if these small changes saved any construction cost as the ships required almost completely new building drawings. ***HMS Opportune*** survived the war and was eventually scrapped at Milford Haven in 1955.

(VT Group)

HMS Brecon, an improved Hunt Class Destroyer on sea trials in the summer of 1942. She and her sister ***HMS Brissenden*** were completed to a Thornycroft modified design with 4ft more beam and 10ft more length which virtually eliminated the stability problems associated with the earlier Hunt Class design.The same 19,000 shp machinery was fitted however which dropped the top speed down to 25 knots. ***HMS Brecon*** served with the Home Fleet until 1943 before moving to the Mediterranean and then the Far East Fleet in 1945. She was placed on the disposal list and scrapped in 1963. *(VT Group)*

Vosper workers assemble marine versions of the Packard Merlin V12 petrol engines for use in MTB's and RAF Rescue launches in the engine assembly shop at the Broad Street yard in Old Portsmouth during WWII. The use of female staff throughout all areas of the yard increased dramatically during WWII as male workers were called to fight. *(VT Group)*

A general view of the Vosper's wooden boat shop at Old Portsmouth during WWII in which a great number of MTB's and RAF Rescue launches were built. The just laid wooden keel in the foreground is for a 73ft RAF Rescue launch and her sister on the adjacent position has just started to have her mahogany skin attached. The covered and lit assembly shed meant that work could proceed un-interrupted by inclement weather and darkness. *(VT Group)*

The improved Type IV Hunt Class Destroyer ***HMS Brissenden*** was launched at Woolston on 15 September 1942 and commissioned only 5 months later on 12 February 1943, such was the urgency for escort warships at this time of the war. She and her sister ***HMS Brecon*** were redesigned by Thornycroft's to give improved stability and the original Hunt Class design proved to be too top heavy. ***HMS Brissenden*** served mainly in home waters until being transferred to the Mediterranean in early 1945. She was placed on the disposal list and scrapped in 1965.
(VT Group)

A 1943 view of the engine shop at Vosper's Old Portsmouth yard showing engine workers completing marine versions of the Packard Merlin V12 petrol engines in rotating assembly jigs for fitment to MTB's and RAF rescue launches. The task of fitting the marine components basically required the whole engine, having been delivered complete from the USA, to be dismantled and rebuilt. *(VT Group)*

The 70ft Vosper's built ***MTB 69*** launches two 21-inch practice torpedoes off the Lulworth coast early in the war. One of 2 similar boats originally built for Greece, she was taken over by the Royal Navy at the outbreak of war. The 45 knot ship was powered by twin Isotta Fraschini V12 petrol engines for high speed and twin Vosper V8's for cruising. She was mainly used for training before being scrapped at the end of the war. *(VT Group)*

The pristine and newly completed modified Black Swan Class Frigate ***HMS Magpie*** on sea trials shortly after completion. Launched at Woolston in March 1943, the steam turbine powered ship was one of 4 similar vessels built by Thornycroft's during WWII. The ship saw war service off the Normandy coast, in the Atlantic and the Arctic and served post war into the 1950's during which she was the command of HRH the Duke of Edinburgh. ***HMS Magpie*** was finally sold for scrapping at Blyth in July 1959. *(VT Group)*

MTB 381 was one of sixteen 73-ft MTB's ordered from Vosper's under the 1943 building programme. Delivered in early 1944, the craft was one of four built at Wivenhoe near Colchester as the Old Portsmouth yard was at full capacity. The three Packard V12 main engines could power the ship at 35 knots and two Vosper V8 engines were also fitted for economical cruising. ***MTB 381*** was heavily armed with four 21-inch torpedo tubes, a twin 29mm gun, a twin rocket projector and twin .303 machine guns. Laid up at the war's end, she was scrapped by 1947. *(VT Group)*

MTB 385 shown running speed trials in the Solent in early 1944. She was another of the sixteen 73ft MTB's ordered from Vosper's under the 1943 building programme, and was built at Wivenhoe. After war service in the western approaches, she was laid up in reserve for a short period before being sold for scrap. *(VT Group)*

A fine view of ***MTB 355*** at speed whilst undergoing contractors speed trials in the Solent. The vessel was one of sixteen ordered under an extension to the 1939 building programme and was delivered from Vosper's Broad Street Yard in early 1942. The 70ft long craft had the almost standard machinery fit of three Packard V12 and twin Vosper V8's which could drive the vessel at 39 knots. She was armed with twin 21-inch torpedo tubes, twin 0.5-inch machine guns and depth charges. ***MTB 355*** was scrapped soon after the war's end.
(VT Group)

Looking up the River Itchen towards the Woolston shipyard fitting out quay at Easter 1944, with the bombed and burnt out Supermarine Spitfire factory in the background. A nearly completed landing craft sits outboard of the modified Black Swan Class Sloop ***HMS Peacock*** and the partially complete destroyers ***Ursa*** and ***Zest***. ***HMS Peacock*** served postwar and was eventually scrapped at Rosyth in 1958. Both ***Ursa*** and ***Zest*** were converted to Type 15 Anti-submarine Frigates in the 1950's and served until they were scrapped in the 1970s. *(VT Group)*

MTB 523 undergoing speed trials in Southampton Water in 1944. She was one of twelve 73ft MTB's ordered from Vosper's under the 1944 building programme. Capable of 36 knots she was powered by the standard fit of three Packard V12 main engines and Vosper V8's for cruising. The vessel was armed with two 18-inch torpedo tubes, a twin 20mm gun, a rocket launcher and twin 0.303 machine guns. Laid up at the end of the war, she was sold for scrapping in 1949. *(VT Group)*

The need for a large number of MTB's and light craft reduced considerably at the war's end, and hundreds were laid up on various rivers and inlets around the country. A row of thirteen MTB's are shown laid up in front of Portchester Castle in the upper reaches of Portsmouth Harbour awaiting disposal. *(VT Group)*

The newly completed Weapons Class Destroyer ***HMS Crossbow*** passing Hythe on Southampton Water soon after commissioning in early 1948. Originally armed with six 4.7-inch guns in twin turrets, the 1980 ton ship was launched at Woolston in December 1945. ***HMS Crossbow*** served with the 6th Flotilla before being placed in reserve in 1955. She was converted to a Radar Picket at Chatham and recommissioned in 1959 for service in home waters. She was paid off again into the reserve in 1963 and was used as a training ship to the marine engineering school ***HMS Sultan***. She was sold for scrap at Briton Ferry in 1972. *(VT Group)*

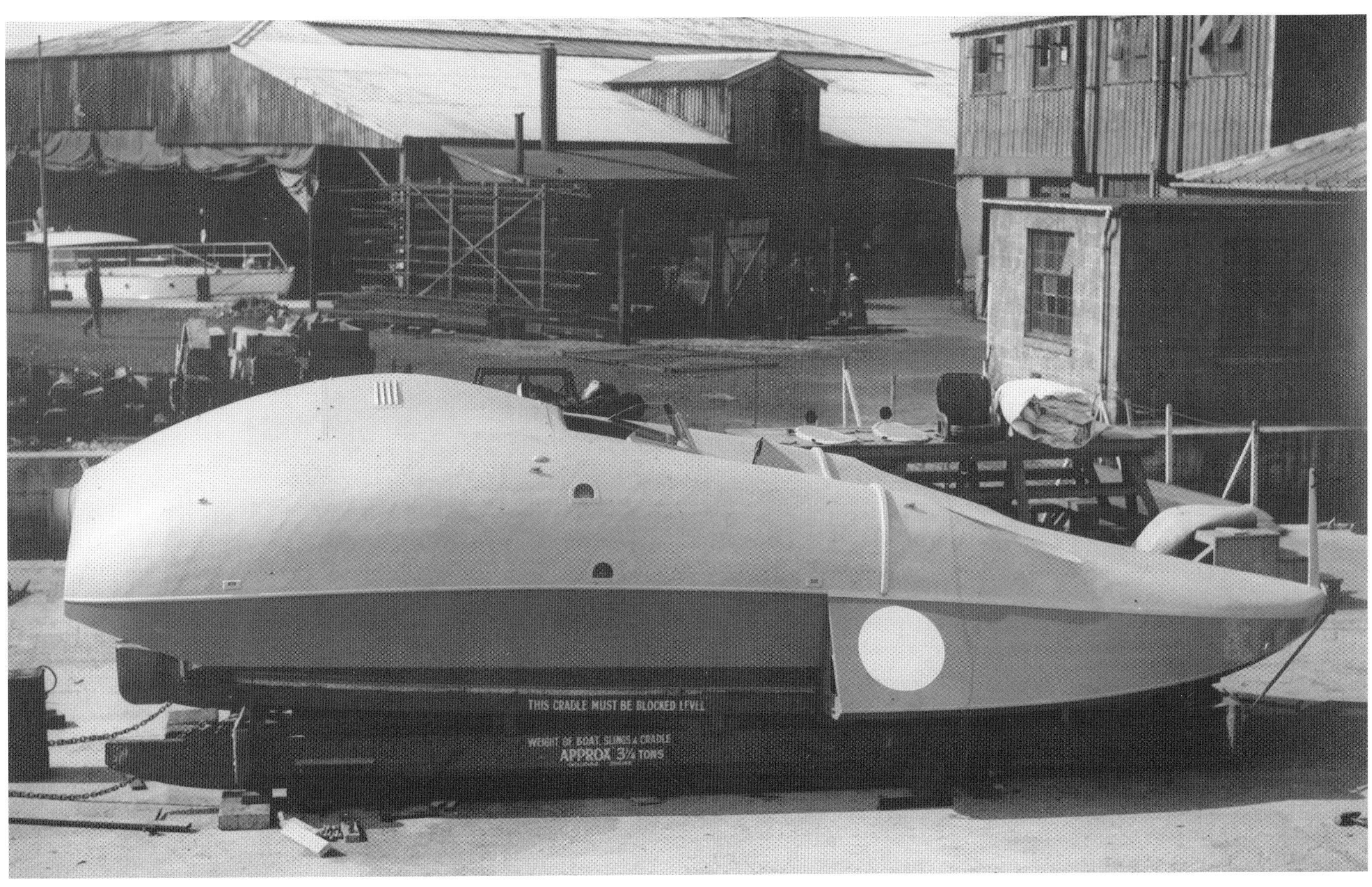

Sir Malcolm Campbell's ***Bluebird K4*** at Portchester in 1947. Originally built of wood in 1938/39 this boat was first powered by a Rolls Royce R Type V12 engine and set a world speed record on Coniston Water in August 1939. In 1947, Vosper's converted the craft to jet power with a De Havilland Goblin engine, but the craft proved unstable at high speed and with the death of Malcolm Campbell in early 1948 his son Donald Campbell had the boat refitted with its original Rolls Royce piston engine. ***Bluebird K4*** eventually sank whilst attempting a new record after hitting a log on Lake Coniston at 170mph in 1951. *(VT Group)*

Wartime experience convinced Vosper's that the virtually standard war time designed hull could be improved upon, most noticeably by modifying the bow so that the chine was higher and the fore sections more deeply veed. The new design was tested in the AEW tank at Haslar and accepted by the Admiralty. The result was the 73ft ***MTB 538*** later to become ***MTB 1601***. The 42 knot Packard engined vessel is seen alongside fitting out at Portchester on 1 September 1948. *(VT Group)*

An early 1948 view of the Vosper's Portchester shipyard which was purchased during the war to compensate for the loss of the Flathouse facility within Portsmouth Naval base which was requisitioned by the Admiralty. The shipyard has been extensively updated and modernised over the years with the addition of covered building berths and a synchro-lift. The VT Group purchased the very successful Halmatic Group in 2001, and moved this company to Portchester. The yard continues to build and overhaul small craft at Portchester. *(VT Group)*

In 1949, Vosper's began a 3 year programme with John Cobb to design and build a new water speed record breaking craft. The result was the unique ***Crusader***, designed for 250mph. This photograph at Portchester shows the small size of the craft with basically a central hull and two outriggers. Although the project ended in disaster and John Cobb was killed, there are good reasons to believe that the basic design was sound and would have achieved its designed speed. *(VT Group)*

An early view of the C Class destroyer ***HMS Concord*** (ex ***Corso***) undergoing full power trials in the English Channel. The ship was launched at Woolston days after the end of the European War and was one of four C Class destroyers built by the Company. She remained in the Far East and served in the Korean War until she paid off in 1957. She was then attached to ***HMS Caledonia*** as a static harbour training ship. She was scrapped at Inverkeithing in Scotland in 1963.

(VT Group)

A general view of Vosper's Broad Street Yard at Old Portsmouth on 10 January 1951 looking across to Portsmouth Naval Base. Herbert Vosper set up his first shipyard in Old Portsmouth in 1871 when he was just 21, and the yard continued to build ships until it closed in the 1986. The site has now been redeveloped into part of the Gunwharf Quay shopping and leisure complex. *(VT Group)*

The Fast Patrol Boat ***HMS Bold Pathfinder*** on the slip at Vosper's Broad Street Yard Old Portsmouth on 28 August 1952. This ship was the Company's first gas turbine powered vessel, being fitted with twin Metro-Vickers G2 engines and twin Mercedes Benz diesels taken from a captured German E-Boat for cruising. This installation was an early example of the combined diesel or gas turbine(CODOG) machinery fit now common in modern warships. The Mercedes engines were later replaced by Napier Deltics. Although not particularly successful ships the designers learnt a great deal about the installation of gas turbines and salt spray ingestion. *(VT Group)*

The Fast Patrol Boat ***HMS Bold Pathfinder*** on sea trials on 18th of February 1953. The hull design of this ship incorporated a round bilge hull, whereas her sistership ***HMS Bold Pioneer*** built by J Samuel Whites on the Isle of White had a hard chine hull shape for a direct comparison. *(VT Group)*

The Daring Class Destroyer ***HMS Duchess*** was built by Thornycroft's at Woolston and completed in October 1952. She was one of the first ships in the RN to have a 440 volt alternating current main electrical system. ***HMS Duchess*** was transferred to the Royal Australian Navy after the loss of ***HMAS Voyager*** in a collision with the Aircraft Carrier ***HMAS Melbourne*** in 1964. ***HMS Duchess*** was eventually purchased for $300,000 in 1972 for conversion into a training ship. Until the completion of the first Type 45 Destroyer ***HMS Daring***, the ***Duchess*** remains the largest destroyer built by the Company. *(VT Group)*

Photographed on trials in the Solent on 17 March 1953, the Fast Patrol Boat ***HMS Gay Bombadier*** was ordered under the Korean War 1951 emergency building programme. Vosper's built 4 of the 73ft boats to an Admiralty design, and they were powered 3 Packard V12 petrol engines. The design was convertible for use as an MTB or Minelayer. The order for these boats came at a critical time for Vosper's as new build work was sparse and the Company was in grave danger of closing. ***HMS Gay Bombadier*** was placed on the disposal list in 1963. *(VT Group)*

The Ham Class Inshore minesweeper ***HMS Popham*** on contractors sea trials in Southampton Water. She was one of eight similiar vessels built by Vosper's at Portsmouth, and a further two were built by Thornycroft at Woolston. The hull was of composite wood and metal construction and the ship displaced 159 tons. One 20mm gun was carried. ***HMS Popham*** was sold to Australia in 1966 for conversion to a diving support ship, but this was not completed and she was sold to commercial interests in February 1976 for $15,000 at Surfers Paradise. *(VT Group)*

The 68ft RAF Crash Tender ***2747*** on trials in Southampton Water. Designed to replace the WWII built Air Sea Rescue Launches, Vosper's based the hull design on the successful ***MTB 1601***. The new boats were powered by marine versions of the Rolls Royce Griffon V12 aero engines used in the later marks of Spitfire and the Shackleton Bomber. The craft were capable of a maximum speed of 40 knots. *(VT Group)*

The Type 14 Anti-submarine Frigate ***HMS Blackwood*** undergoing contractors trials in Southampton Water in the summer of 1957. Built by Thornycroft's at Woolston, she was one of 12 similar ships completed for the RN as 2nd rate Frigates. During 1958/59 her hull was strengthened after cracks were found due to the severe weather conditions encountered on fishery protection duties around Iceland. The ships were unusual for RN service in that they had only one propeller to give a speed of 24 knots. She was placed on the disposal list in the mid 1970's and scrapped. *(VT Group)*

In 1959, Vosper's built as a private venture the prototype Fast Patrol Boat ***Ferocity***. Developed with the help of a quarter scale model, the 88ft long vessel was powered by two Bristol Siddley Proteus gas turbines and incorporated deep V sections forward to give improved sea keeping. ***Ferocity*** had a top speed of over 50 knots. As a prototype she was a success and justified the financial outlay as boats with a similar form were later ordered from the Company by Germany, Denmark, Malaysia, Brunei and Libya.

(VT Group)

The Fast Patrol Boat ***HMS Brave Borderer*** was built by Vosper's at Portsmouth and completed in 1960. The 96ft long hull had an aluminium framework clad in a double mahogany skin, and sheathed in glass fibre below the water line. The craft was powered by three Bristol Siddley gas turbines driving super cavitating propellers which could drive her at 50 knots. After a relatively short service life, ***HMS Brave Borderer*** was discarded in the 1970's. *(VT Group)*

The Type 12 Anti-submarine Frigate ***HMNZS Otago*** was completed at Thornycroft's Woolston shipyard in June 1960. The ship was originally ordered for the Royal Navy as ***HMS Hastings***, but was transferred to New Zealand whilst still building. As completed, she was generally similar to the RN Type 12's but was slightly modified to suit New Zealand conditions. She was discarded and scrapped in 1983. *(VT Group)*

The Fast Patrol Boat ***HMS Brave Borderer*** and her sister ***Brave Swordsman*** were designed for offensive operations against enemy warships and merchant ships in coastal, inshore and shoal waters where high speed is essential. The 90ft long craft displaced 114 tons and were originally armed with a 3.3-inch gun turret specially designed for this application, twin 21-inch torpedo tubes and one 40mm gun. Both vessels were initially in the Coastal Forces Trials and Special Service Squadron based at ***HMS Hornet***, Gosport and in 1962 were attached to the Fisheries Protection Squadron for which their high speed made them eminently suitable.

(VT Group)

The newly completed Type 81 Tribal Class general purpose Frigate ***HMS Gurkha*** photographed in the Solent in 1963. Fully air-conditioned, and designed for service in such areas as the Persian Gulf, the ships were powered by a COSAG arrangement of one steam turbine and a single Metrovick gas turbine driving a single propeller for 28 knots. ***HMS Gurkha*** was in the reserve standby squadron in 1982 when the Falklands War started, and she was brought forward for further RN service. In 1985 she refitted at Woolston and was sold to Indonesia as the ***Wilhelmus Zakarias Yohannes***. *(VT Group)*

One of six 110ft diesel engined Fast Patrol Boats for Peru on the building slip at Vosper's yard in Old Portsmouth in 1964. Of steel construction, the hull design featured a round bilge form although at high speed these boats still began to plane and had pronounced knuckles in the forebody to deflect spray. Two were transferred to the Coast Guard in 1975 and the remaining four were stricken between 1982-1990. *(VT Group)*

An aerial view of the Vosper Thornycroft Singapore shipyard with the RN Ton Class Minesweeper ***HMS Essington*** just coming alongside for maintenance. Another Ton class vessel is out of the water on the quayside undergoing deep repair. ***HMS Essington*** was transferred to the Malaysian Navy in 1964. The loss making Singapore yard was sold soon after the Company returned to the private sector in 1985. *(VT Group)*

A general view of the Woolston shipyard showing the construction of the new fitting out quay on 30 January 1964 with the Southampton based Red Funnel Line tug ***Calshot*** fitting out alongside. This was a time of lean orders for J.I. Thornycroft's but the Company invested wisely in providing improved shipbuilding facilities and machinery and vastly longer fitting out quays. This put them in a good negotiating position when the opportunity came to join forces with Vosper Ltd. *(VT Group)*

Construction workers reinforcing the shoring of the new fitting out quay at Woolston on 22 May 1964. The new longer fitting out quay provided much needed extra alongside capacity, and it remained in use until the Woolston shipyard completed its last ship in 2004. *(VT Group)*

The launch of the Royal Danish Navy Soloven Class Motor Torpedo Boat ***Soloven*** at Vosper's Portchester shipyard in April 1963.The design was a combination of the Brave Class and the Ferocity type construction. Six vessels of the class were ordered, two were built at Portchester with the remaining four built at the Royal Dockyard Copenhagen with Vosper's assistance. The entire class was discarded in 1990/1991. *(VT Group)*

The Royal Danish Navy Soloven Class Motor Torpedo Boat ***Soloven*** undergoing contractors speed trials in Southampton Water in the summer of 1964. The craft was powered by three Bristol Siddley Proteus gas turbines which could drive the ship at 54 knots, with General Motors diesels on the wing propeller shafts for cruising. The 96 ft long vessel was armed with four 21" torpedo tubes and two 40mm Bofors anti-aircraft guns. *(VT Group)*

The Vosper built Mk1 Corvette ***Kromantse*** was delivered to Ghana in July 1964. The steel hulled ship is shown on contractors sea trials in the English Channel in late June 1964. Her sister ship ***Keta*** was built by Vickers. The twin Maybach diesels gave the vessel a speed of 18 knots. ***Kromantse*** was the largest ship built at the Camber yard Old Portsmouth up to 1964, and stretched the shipyard to maximum capacity, eventually forcing Vosper's to look for additional building space. The result was the approach to merge with the Southampton shipbuilder J.I. Thornycroft 2 years later. *(VT Group)*

The exercise Minelayer ***HMS Abdiel*** was ordered from Thornycroft's at Woolston in June 1965 and launched in January 1967. A one off ship, she displaced 1430 tons and was powered by twin 1345hp Paxman Ventura 16 cylinder diesels. The ship was designed to support mine counter measure forces and to lay exercise mine, for which she had a capacity of 44. After a relatively short service life, she was prematurely discarded in 1988. *(VT Group)*

An aerial view of the Vosper's Broad Street yard in July 1965 shows a 177ft long Corvette for Ghana under construction on the slip- way, and two nearly complete 110ft Fast Patrol Boats for Peru alongside the fitting out berth. The tight confines of the yard can be clearly seen which limited the length of vessel that could be built. In addition modern shipbuilding techniques required a covered berth, space for which was not available at the site. As a consequence, the yard closed soon after the Company was privatised and returned to the private sector in 1986. *(VT Group)*

Four Thornycroft built vessels are shown in this aerial view of the newly completed Woolston fitting out quay on the 18th of April 1966. The Leander Class Frigate ***HMS Juno*** sits inboard of the two just launched Gosport Ferries ***Portsmouth Queen*** and ***Gosport Queen***, and the 1962 built Southampton Corporation diesel engined Floating Bridge is about to depart from Woolston for the Southampton side. *(VT Group)*

The 96ft Malaysian Fast Patrol Boat ***Perkasa*** was launched by Vosper's in April 1966. One of a Class of four, she was based on the private venture craft ***Ferocity***. Her three Proteus gas turbines were capable of propelling the craft at 54 knots, with twin General Motors diesels on the wing shafts fitted for cruising. The hull is entirely of glued wooden construction with aluminium upperworks. *(VT Group)*

The Leander Class Frigate ***HMS Juno*** was completed at Woolston in July 1967. The Frigate was taken in hand at Rosyth Naval Base in 1981 for conversion into a sea going training ship for marine engineers and navigators, but economic constraints forced a long delay and the refit was not completed until 1985. For her training task, all armament was removed and the space below the 4.5-inch turret converted to classrooms. ***HMS Juno*** was discarded for scrap in 1992. *(VT Group)*

The Libyan Maintenance Repair ship ***Zeltin*** was built at Woolston and delivered in January 1969. A novel ship, she was designed to support small surface vessels such as fast patrol craft and had a 41m x 12m well deck that could be flooded to a depth of 2.3m. The well deck is swept by a movable 3 ton crane with an additional 9 ton crane on the port side to support the workshop. The 2200 ton ship is powered by twin Paxman Ventura 16 cylinder diesels. *(VT Group)*

The ex Royal Navy Battle Class Destroyer ***HMS Sluys*** was refitted by Thornycroft's at Woolston and transferred to the Imperial Iranian Navy in 1969. Renamed ***Artemiz***, she was substantially updated and modernised for service in the Persian Gulf. ***Artemiz*** survived the fall of the Shah of Iran in 1979 to continue in service with the Revolutionary Guard for a number of years. The ship was refitted in South Africa during 1975/76 and was renamed ***Damavand*** in 1985. She was discarded in the 1990's. *(VT Group)*

The GRP prototype Minehunter ***HMS Wilton*** undergoing trials in Southampton Water. Ordered in 1970, and based on the design of a Ton Class wooden hulled ship, ***HMS Wilton*** used the equipment and machinery from the discarded ***HMS Derriton***, the hull of which had succumbed to the ravages of time. Building in GRP required clean dry and relatively stable temperature conditions, not available with an outside berth, so a new covered building berth was constructed at Woolston. This covered facility was later used to build the Hunt and Sandown Class GRP Minehunters. *(VT Group)*

In 1970, Vosper's at Portchester completed three Scimitar Class Fast training Boats for the Royal Navy, ***HM Ships Scimitar***, ***Sabre*** and ***Cutlass***. Fitted with twin Proteus gas turbines and twin Foden diesels in a CODOG arrangement, and constructed of wood, these boats had a modified hull form with a longer bow overhang and some Vee remaining at the transom. All three attended the 1977 Silver Jubilee Review and in 1979 ***Scimitar*** went to Hong Kong for Anti-immigration duties. They were all sold commercially to Greek owners in 1991. *(VT Group)*

The Iranian Mk 5 Frigate ***Saam*** undertaking contractors sea trials in the English Channel in June 1970. One of two built at Woolston, her sister ***Faramarz*** was sunk by US forces in April 1988. When first built, these frigates were the fastest major warships in the world achieving 39 knots with a CODOG machinery fit of Twin RR Olympus gas turbines and twin Paxman Ventura diesels drivingVosper developed super cavitating propellers. The ship was renamed ***Alvand*** after the 1979 Islamic Revolution. *(VT Group)*

The Nigerian Navy Mk 3 Corvette ***Dorina*** on contractors sea trials off the Spithead Forts in 1972. One of two ships of the class built at Portsmouth, the 650 ton vessel was powered by twin MAN diesels. The ***Dorina*** was in a poor material condition by April 1987 due to indifferent maintenance and a complete lack of funds and subsequently sank at her moorings. She was eventually raised and now serves as a damage control ship at Sapele. A sad end to what was a very good and handy ship.

(VT Group)

The Libyan Mk 7 Frigate ***Dat Assawari*** on contractors sea trials late in 1972. The Woolston built ship was delivered to Libya in February 1973, and displaced 1650 tons.. She was powered by a CODOG arrangement of twin RR Olympus gas turbines and Paxman Ventura diesels driving controllable pitch propellers. ***Dat Assawari*** was damaged by bombs in 1980 and was sent for refitting at Genoa in Italy, but did not return to Libya until 1985. By 1989 she was once again in a poor material condition and returned to Italy again for a further refit in 1991. *(VT Group)*

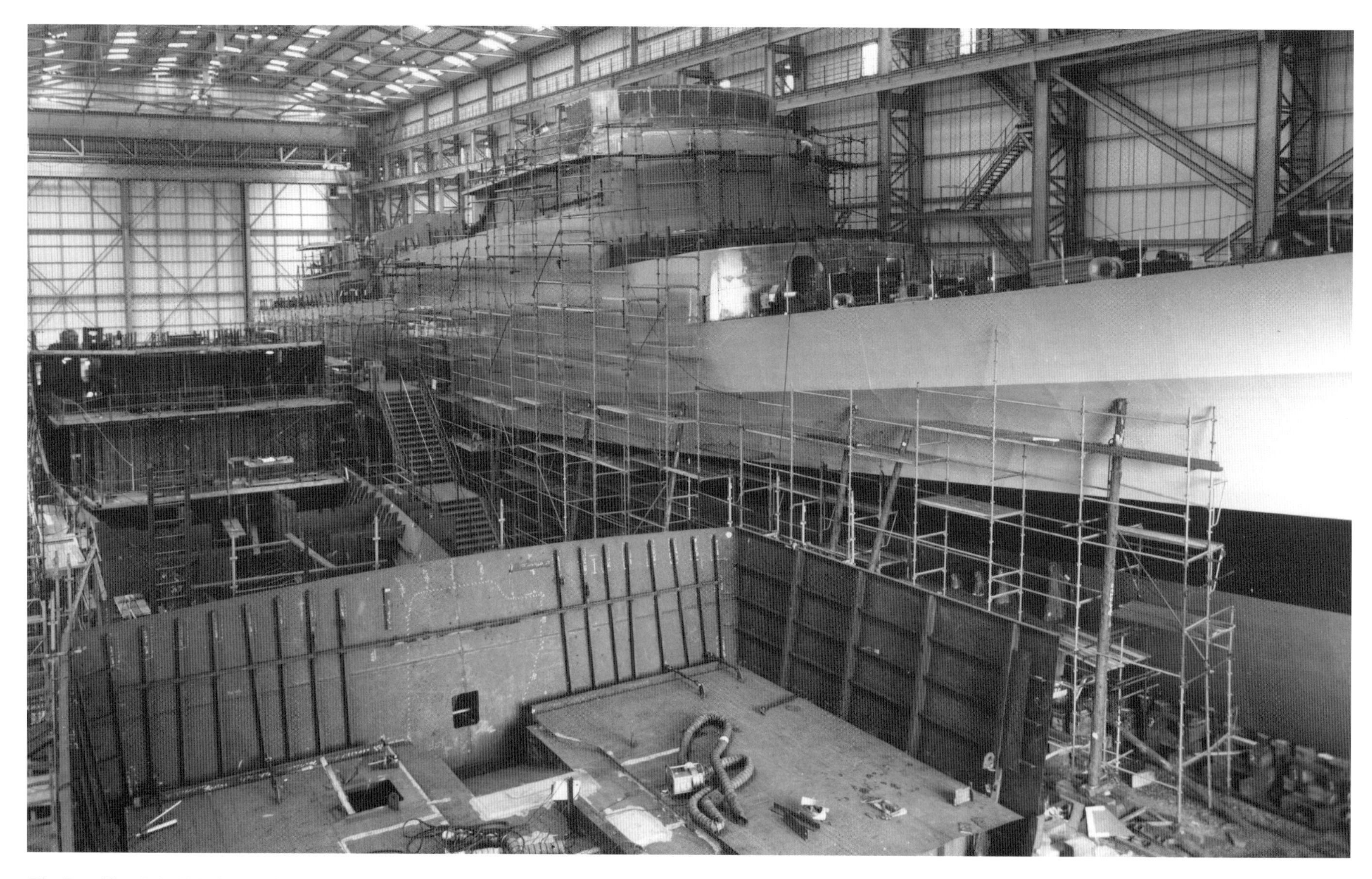

The Brazilian Mk 10 Frigate ***Niteroi*** in the main shipbuilding assembly hangar at Woolston in early January 1974. The ship was launched one month later on 8 February and completed in November 1976. She was the first of a class of six contracted to VT, with the first four being built at Woolston and the remaining two being built at Rio de Janerio with VT providing a technology transfer and building advice. The covered building berth at Woolston was funded using this prestigious order. The 3,800 ton Mk 10 Frigates were powered with a CODOG machinery fit of twin RR Olympus gas turbines and MTU 16 cylinder diesels driving controllable pitch propellers.

(VT Group)

The Woolston built Type 21 frigate ***HMS Amazon*** comes alongside her sister ship ***HMS Antelope*** which is still flying the Red Ensign and on contractors sea trials in the English Channel. Except for the trials ship ***HMS Exmouth***, ***HMS Amazon*** was the first RN ship to go to sea with the now ubiquitous Rolls Royce Olympus/Tyne COGOG gas turbine machinery fit, and as such, experienced many of the early problems associated with this installation. As a result of hull cracking brought about by the severe weather conditions in the South Atlantic, she was strengthened with double plates amidships in 1983. Along with her five surviving sisters, ***HMS Amazon*** was sold to Pakistan in the mid 1990's. *(VT Group)*

The busy Woolston fitting out quay in 1976 with the two Brazillian Mk 10 Frigates ***BNS Niteroi*** and ***Defensora*** ahead on the second Type 21 Frigate built by the Company ***HMS Antelope***. The Mk 10 was a development of the Type 21, but the Brazillian ships were considerably bigger as can be seen in this photograph. The new large covered building berth, funded by the Brazillian order is also shown to good effect. *(VT Group)*

The Type 21 Frigate ***HMS Antelope*** still flying the Red Ensign on trials in July 1975. She was the second of three Type 21 Frigates built by the Company at Woolston for the Royal Navy. Damaged by unexploded bombs dropped by Argentinean A4 Skyhawks in the1982 Falkland War, she retired to San Carlos Water to enable bomb disposal experts to try and defuse the bombs. Unfortunately one exploded causing uncontrollable fires and eventually the magazine exploded and the ship was lost on 25 April. *(VT Group)*

The Patrol Boat ***Barzan*** was one of six similar 103ft long vessels built by Vosper's at Portchester for the Gulf state of Qatar in 1975. A relatively simple design, the steel hulled ships had a twin 30mm gun and were powered by Paxman Valenta diesels. The ships were completed at a particularly busy time for the Company as both the Portsmouth and Portchester yards were at full capacity also building six ships for Abu Dhabi. *(VT Group)*

The almost complete bow module for the Type 42 Destroyer ***HMS Southampton*** is being positioned ready for welding to the main hull structure inside the ship assembly hangar at Woolston in the autumn of 1978. Although a tight fit, the covered shipbuilding hall was large enough to build ***HMS Southampton*** and ***HMS Nottingham*** side by side, and the protection afforded from the weather allowed advanced fitting out before the upper decks were sealed.
(VT Group)

The Ton Class wooden hulled Minesweeper ***HMS Hubberston*** high and dry on the Portchester syncro-lift for hull cleaning and painting. The 800 ton capacity lift was installed along with a new wet dock in 1978 whilst the Company was still a part of British Shipbuilders, and allowed vessels to be moved in and out of the covered Number 4 shed building and repair facility along a three track railway line. *(VT Group)*

The first Hunt class Mine Counter Measures Vessel, ***HMS Brecon***, alongside the Woolston fitting out berth not long after launching in the autumn of 1978. The ship was accepted into service on 21 March 1980 and was powered by two Ruston-Paxman Deltic diesels. A further Deltic drove a 525kw alternator for magnetic minesweeping or four hydraulic pumps used to drive the ship during slow speed running. Two Foden diesel generators were used to power the ship's other electrical services. The ship was later transferred to Greece as part of an agreement for VT to supply four Super Vita Fast Attack Craft in conjunction with the Elefis Shipyard in Athens. *(VT Group)*

The prefabricated stern section module hangs on the overhead crane inside the Woolston covered assembly building prior to attachment to the Type 42 Destroyer ***HMS Southampton*** on the building slip in the summer of 1978. The stern module had been constructed in another building at the yard and moved by trolley and cranes to the assembly hangar for attachment to the ship. *(VT Group)*

The Type 42 Destroyers ***HMS Southampton*** on the left and ***HMS Nottingham*** under construction inside the main assembly building at Woolston in the autumn of 1978. The hull of the ***HMS Nottingham*** is still open and shows the inner hull construction and long propeller shaft tunnels. The covered building facility enables year long working devoid of inclement weather conditions and more comprehensive fitting out with machinery and equipment before the hull decks are sealed.

(VT Group)

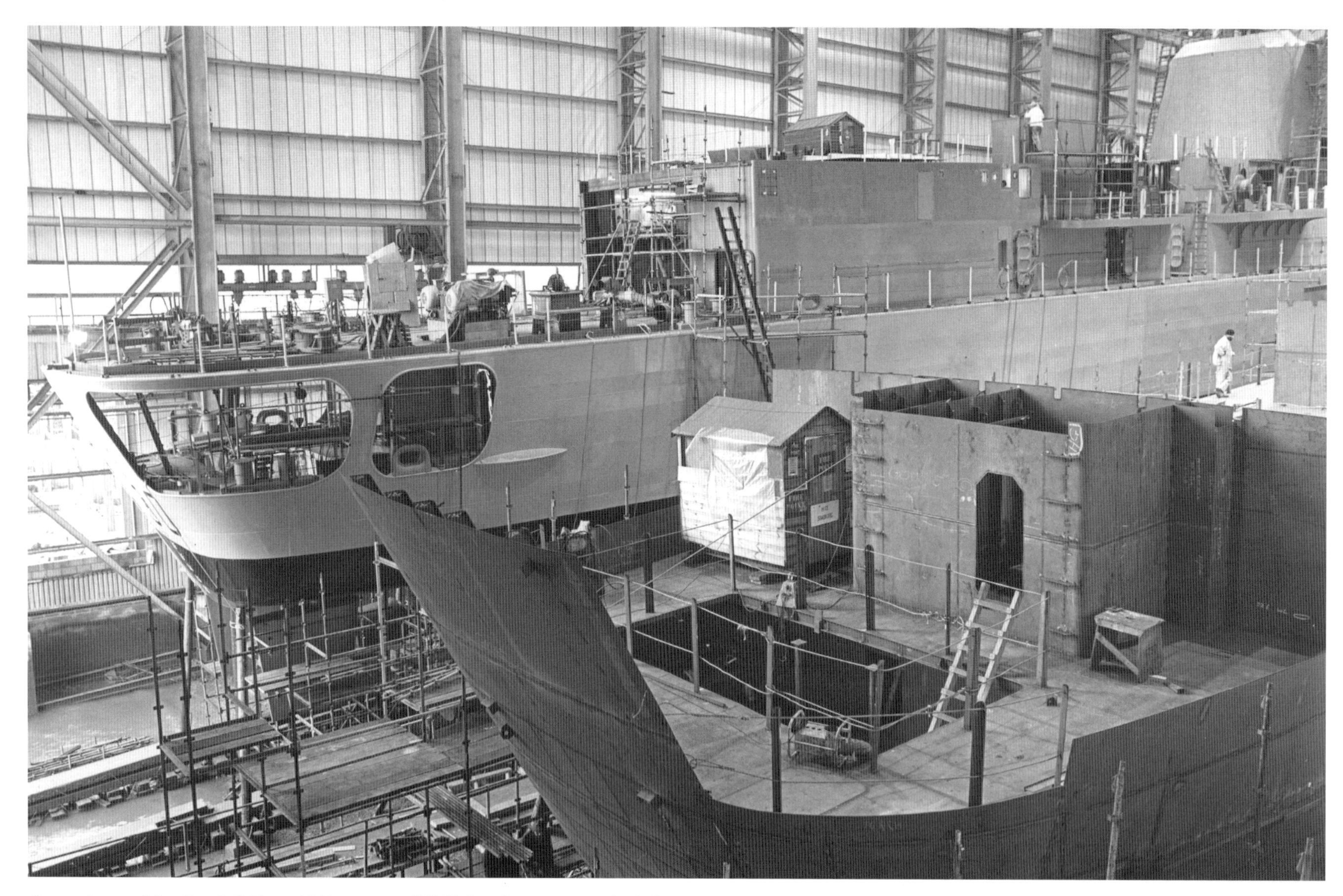

Stern views of the Batch 2 Type 42 Destroyers ***HMS Southampton*** on the left and her sister ***HMS Nottingham*** inside the main assembly hangar at Woolston in November 1978. ***HMS Southampton*** was laid down in October 1976 and has now been painted ready for launching in January 1979. The first prefabricated hull section for ***HMS Nottingham*** was assembled on the building slip on 6 February 1978. *(VT Group)*

The Batch 2 Type 42 Destroyer ***HMS Southampton*** was launched at midnight on 29 January 1979 by management staff after industrial action by the shipyard workers prevented the ship being launched during the naming ceremony earlier in the day. Delivered to the Royal Navy in July 1981, she was still on trials during the Falklands war, but was rushed to completion and deployed south in the first batch of reinforcements. ***HMS Southampton*** was badly damaged and nearly cut in two in a collision with the container ship ***Tor Bay*** in the Persian Gulf in September 1988 and had to be returned to the UK for repair aboard the heavy lift ship ***Mighty Servant***. The ship was repaired by Swan Hunter on the Tyne, returning to service in May 1992. *(VT Group)*

The first prefabricated hull modules for the Batch 3 stretched Type 42 Destroyer ***HMS Gloucester*** are laid inside the covered building berth at Woolston on 25 October 1979, on the slip vacated earlier in the year by ***HMS Southampton***. The ship would be launched three years later in November 1982. The ship occupying the other berth is the Batch 2 Type 42, ***HMS Nottingham***, which would be launched just four months later in February 1980. The covered building berth was financed alongside the Brazilian Mk10 Frigate purchase and enabled the Company to build two Type 42 sized ships side by side. *(VT Group)*

Manned by Company personnel, the first Hunt Class Mine Counter Measures Vessel, ***HMS Brecon***, proceeds down the River Itchen, from her birthplace at Woolston, to be handed over to the Royal Navy at ***HMS Vernon***, Portsmouth on 6 December 1979. The 60 metre long ship weighs 625 tons and at the time was the largest glass reinforced plastic (GRP) warship in the world. Alongside the fitting out quay can be seen the second of the class, ***HMS Ledbury***, which was launched the day before. *(VT Group)*

An aerial view of the Broad street yard at Old Portsmouth in late 1980 showing the 56m Fast Missile Craft ***SNV Dhofar*** building for Oman on the building slip. The tight constraints of the entrance to the yard can be clearly seen which limited the size of vessel that could be built there. The site was sold soon after privatisation in 1986 and has since been redeveloped as part of the Gunwharf shopping and retail complex. *(VT Group)*

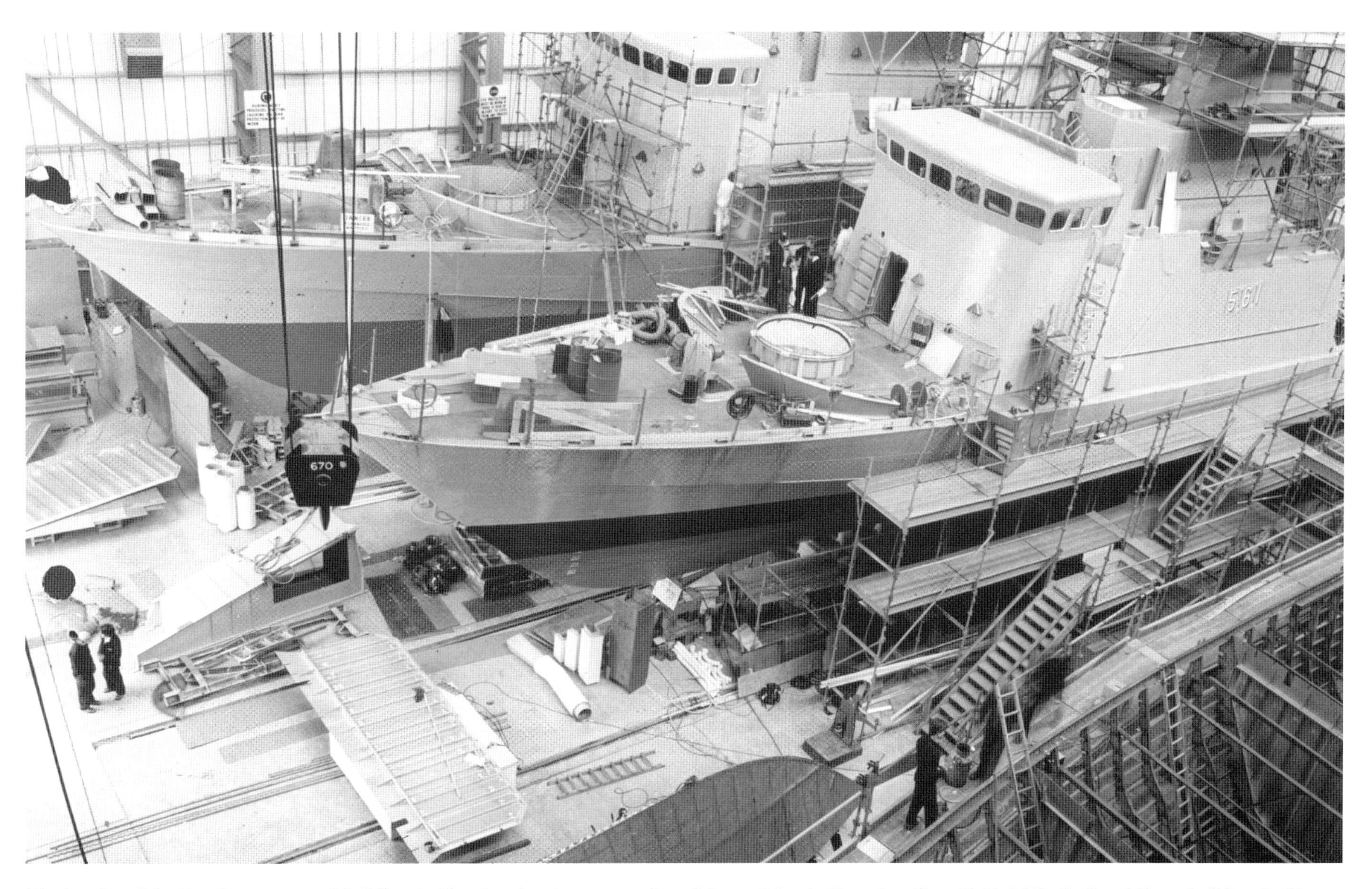

The interior of the Portchester covered building facility showing the construction of three of the six Ramadan Class Guided Missile Patrol Boats building for Eygpt. Ordered in 1977, the first pair were delivered to Eygpt in 1981, and the last pair in December 1982. The hulls were constructed of steel with a riveted aluminium superstructure, and the four MTU V20 diesels drove 4 shafts to give a speed of 40 knots. *(VT Group)*

The Egyptian Ramadan Class Guided Missile Fast Patrol Boat ***Ramadan*** at high speed on contractors sea trials off the Isle of Wight in 1980. She was the lead ship in a class of six, all built at VT's Portchester shipyard, and is heavily armed with an Oto Melara 76mm compact gun system, a twin 40mm Breda anti-aircraft gun turret, and four Otomat anti-ship missiles. The ship is also fitted with a Ferranti CAAIS automated data system. She is still in service with the Eygptian Navy. *(VT Group)*

The launch of the Batch 2 Type 42 destroyer ***HMS Nottingham*** at Woolston on 18th of February 1980. She was completed in December 1982 and commissioned for service in April 1983. The ship was severely damaged by grounding at Lord Howe Island off the Eastern Australian coast in July 2002 and had to be returned to the UK by heavy lift ship. ***HMS Nottingham*** was subsequently repaired by Fleet Support Ltd, a company jointly owned by VT and BAE Systems at Portsmouth at a cost of £26m, and returned to operational service in the summer of 2004. *(VT Group)*

A fine view of the Woolston fitting out quay taken from the Itchen Bridge in 1981 showing the Batch 2 Type 42 Destroyer ***HMS Southampton*** outboard of her newly launched sister ship ***HMS Nottingham***. The nearly complete Hunt Class MCMV ***HMS Hurworth*** lays upriver. The immense size of the covered ship assembly hangar, which dominates the Woolston skyline can be clearly seen. *(VT Group)*

The brand new Batch 2 Type 42 Destroyer ***HMS Southampton*** proceeds slowly down Southampton Water on the first day of her contractors sea trials in the summer of 1981 crowded on the upper deck with RN and VT personnel. The clean lines of the ship can be clearly seen, and she is still riding high in the water as additional equipment has yet to be fitted. The ship was delivered to the RN on 23 July 1981. *(VT Group)*

HMS Dulverton, the fifth Hunt Class Mine Counter Measures Vessel built by VT for the Royal Navy slides down the ways into the River Itchen from the GRP assembly building after launching by the ship's sponsor, Mrs Edna Jaffray, wife of the Under Secretary of State for the Navy, on 3rd November 1982. The ship was commissioned for service just one year later in November 1983. She later deployed to the Arabian Sea with others of her class during the 1991 Gulf War and served with distinction, being credited with the destruction of a large number of mines. *(VT Group)*

HMS Gloucester takes to the water at Woolston for the first time on 2 November 1982. The launch was something of a turning point for the Company in that she was the last large steel ship built at Woolston for almost 18 years until the Research Vessel Tri-maran ***Triton*** was launched in May 2000. ***HMS Gloucester*** was the largest vessel constructed inside the covered building berth which had to be extended out towards Victoria Road. The limiting width of the River Itchen can be clearly seen and was one of the prime reasons for moving the shipbuilding facility to Portsmouth. Although she looks almost complete, a considerable amount of equipment has still to be installed, and fitting out would take another two years. The ship was finally commissioned on 11 September 1985. *(VT Group)*

The busy fitting out quay at Woolston in the summer of 1985. The almost complete stretched Type 42 Destroyer ***HMS Gloucester*** sits against the quay inside of the Type 81 Tribal Class Frigate ***Hasanuddin*** (ex ***HMS Tartar***) being refitted after sale to Indonesia. Outboard of the ***Hasanuddin*** lies the Hunt Class MCMV ***HMS Hurworth*** which commissioned on 2nd of July 1985. Upriver is the Algerian Landing Ship Logistic ***Kalaat Beni Rached*** the hull of which was built by VT at Woolston under sub-contract to Brooke Marine at Lowestoft. *(VT Group)*

The stretched Type 42 Destroyer ***HMS Gloucester*** on contractors sea trials in the English Channel in the summer of 1985. The ship is one of four improved Type 42's with a 16m increase in length to provide improved levels of sea-worthiness, endurance and habitability. As a result of additional weight growth and hull cracking, she has received hull strengthening strakes amidships. The ship fought with distinction in the first Gulf War destroying an Iraqi Silkworm missile that was heading for the American Battleship ***USS Missouri***. *(VT Group)*

Another view of the Woolston fitting out quay looking towards Southampton Water in the late summer of 1985, with the almost complete Hunt Class MCMV ***HMS Hurworth*** outside of her newly launched sister ***HMS Bicester***. Down river are the two ex-RN Type 81 Tribal Class Frigates (ex ***HMS Gurkha***) which was built by Thornycroft's in 1963, and ***Hasanuddin*** (ex-***HMS Tartar***) refitting after sale to Indonesia. *(VT Group)*

The 56m Guided Missile Patrol Boat ***Umoja*** was one of two Nyayo Class built at the Portchester shipyard and delivered to Kenya at the end of March 1988. Generally similar to earlier Province Class vessels built for Oman and Eygpt, the craft are armed with an Oto Melara 76mm compact gun system, four Otomat anti-ship missiles and twin 30mm Oerlikon/BMARC guns. The Kenyan vessels are powered by 4 Paxman Valenta diesels with electric motors used for slow speed patrolling. The vessel carries a high speed semi-rigid inspection boat on the stern. *(VT Group)*

A Sandown Class Single Role Mine Hunter (SRMH) hull mould in the GRP assembly building at Woolston. The single skinned hull is layered by hand in the mould and largely fitted out with equipment and machinery before the hull decks are sealed. The Sandown Class were the first RN ships to be completely designed and drawn on the new Computer Aided Design (CAD) system installed at the Woolston shipyard. All of the 12 Sandown Class ships ordered by the RN have been built at Woolston.
(VT Group)

A pre-assembled superstructure module for the Sandown Class SRMH ***HMS Grismby*** being lowered into position on the hull inside the GRP assembly building at Woolston in late 1997. The main hull is still in the mould and the main strengthening members on the hull sides and bulkheads can be clearly seen. The main engines and much of the hull equipment have yet to be installed. The ship was launched less than 9 months later in August 1998. *(VT Group)*

HMS Sandown was the first of the 12 ship Sandown Class Single Role Minehunters built at Woolston. The Glass Reinforced Plastic(GRP) construction vessels are pure minehunters with no minesweeping capability. The machinery consists of twin Paxman Valenta diesels and twin Rolls Royce CV8 generators that can be coupled to the Voith Schneider vertical cycloidal propulsors for quiet running during mine hunting. Two electric motors power the twin bow thrusters that are used for dynamic positioning. ***HMS Sandown*** was laid down in February 1987 and delivered to the RN in June 1989. *(VT Group)*

Seen running contractors sea trials in the English Channel in January 1989 the Omani 56m Province Class Guided Missile Fast Attack Craft ***Mussandam*** was the last of four similar vessels built for the Gulf State at the Company's Portchester Shipyard. Ordered in January 1986, she was launched in March 1988 and delivered to the Royal Navy of Oman in March 1989. The four Paxman Valenta diesels drive 4 shafts and the craft can achieve 38 knots. She is heavily armed with an Oto Melara 76mm compact gun system, Exocet anti-ship missiles and a twin Breda 40mm gun turret. *(VT Group)*

Looking up river towards the Itchen Bridge, the 56m Qatar Guided Missile Fast Strike Craft ***Barzan*** takes to the water for the first time at Woolston on 1 April 1995. The steel hulled vessel is already approximately 75% complete with the majority of her weapons including the 76mm Oto Melara gun, the Sadral missile launcher, Goalkeeper Close in Weapon System (CIWS) and associated sensors already aboard. Completion and crew training before delivery to the Gulf State would take a further year.

(VT Group)

The third of class Guided Missile Fast Strike Craft for Qatar emerges from the covered construction facility at Woolston on 1 August 1996. The advanced build state of the vessel on launching reflects the modular construction methods that can be deployed with a covered assembly facility, although this vessel has been sent down the ways without her Goalkeeper CIWS. The ship is powered by four MTU V20 diesels that drive four fixed pitch propellers to give a maximum speed of 35 knots. She arrived in the Gulf in 1998. *(VT Group)*

In 1992, the Company secured an order against intense competition for the construction of two 83m Corvettes for the Gulf State of Oman. The first of these heavily armed Muheet Class vessels is shown on launching at Woolston in 1997. The ship carries an Oto Melara 76mm compact gun system, an 8 round Crotale anti-aircraft missile system and 8 Exocet anti-ship missiles. The 1,450 ton ships are powered by Crossley Pielstick 16 cylinder diesels and have a flight deck large enough to operate a Super Puma helicopter.
(VT Group)

The SRMH, ***HMS Pembroke*** is launched at Woolston on 12 December 1997. Clearly visible in this view is the bow launching cradle that would be removed after launching, the long bilge keels and the twin Voith Schneider propulsors. As the SRMH programme progressed vessels were launched in a more advanced state of completion - compare this picture with that of ***HMS Shoreham's*** launch on page 144. *(VT Group)*

An aerial view of the Woolston shipyard in 1998 showing the large covered shipbuilding facility, and down river the two GRP assembly buildings with their launching ways extending into the River Itchen that were used to build the Hunt Class MCMV and Sandown SRMH. Alongside the fitting out quay are the two nearly complete Muheet Class Corvettes for the State of Oman and two of the four 56m Fast Strike Craft for Oman. *(VT Group)*

Two newly completed 56m Fast Strike Craft for the Gulf State of Qatar high and dry on the Portchester snycro-lift for hull cleaning and maintenance prior to delivery. Four vessels were ordered in 1992 and all were built at Woolston. The Company's Portchester syncro-lift provides a unique and cost affective docking operation as up to the construction of the new shipbuilding yard within Portsmouth Naval Base with its attached dry docks, it was the only Company owned docking facility. *(VT Group)*

A stern view of the 83m Corvette ***Qahir Al - Amwaj*** built for the Gulf State of Oman on contractors speed trials in the English Channel in 1999. The large flight deck capable of landing a Super Puma helicopter is shown to good effect. The two ships of this class are some of the most heavily armed ships of their type in the Persian Gulf area and provided the Royal Navy of Oman with a significant upgrade in their offensive and defensive capability. *(VT Group)*

The Royal Navy of Oman 83m Missile Corvette ***Qahir Al Amwaj*** on sea trials in the Solent in 1999, one of two built by VT at Woolston. These heavily armed ships carry an Oto Melara rapid gun system, an 8 round Crotale anti-aircraft missile system, and 8 Exocet anti-ship missiles. The ships displace 1450 tons and are powered by twin Crossley Piestick diesels. *(VT Group)*

The 115ft long ***Cable and Wireless Challenger*** under construction at the top end of the main ship assembly hangar at Woolston in 1997. The GRP hulled craft was designed to break the round the world power boat record previously held by the US nuclear submarine ***Triton***. The record attempt took in 15 stops for fuel and provisioning and beat the previous attempt by more than 8 days. The Nigel Irens designed tri-maran craft was powered by twin 350hp Cummins diesels and took 74 days and 20 hours to complete the successful attempt. *(VT Group)*

A computer generated view of the advanced Sea Wraith stealth ship design actively marketed by the Company in 1997/98. The design used advanced features such as multi-facetted and smooth panels without right angles to achieve its stealthy profile. The ship also featured a novel wave piercing bow design. Although the ship never sold, many of the advanced design features on the ship have since found their way into the Type 45 Destroyer design. *(VT Group)*

Built by the Halmatic Division at Portchester, the Very Fast Vessel (VSV) has been delivered to the UK Royal Marines and other special forces. The VSV hull, deck and superstructure are of a deep foam cored monocoque sandwich construction with carbon fibre and kevlar skins in a matrix of epoxy resin. The twin diesels of 650hp give a speed in excess of 50 knots. *(VT Group)*

The experimental Tri-maran ***RV Triton*** undergoing sea trials on 28 July 2000. The stability of the Tri-maran hull form with very little heel under a tight turn can be clearly seen. The revolutionary 90m long ship was launched almost 97% complete, and the Tri-maran hull form with its reduced waterplane area requires almost one third less installed horsepower compared to a monohull design of comparable size to maintain the same speed. The ship featured a novel diesel electric propulsion system with a single large propeller on the centre hull and two small propellers on the side pod hulls. She was built to demonstrate the Tri-maran concept and the data produced will be used to formulate the design for the new Royal Navy Surface Combatant (FSC). *(VT Group)*

The last of the SRMH's, ***HMS Shoreham***, was launched at Woolston on 9 April 2001 by Lady Perowne. The twin Voith Schneider vertical cycloidal propulsors are clearly visible at the stern and the ship has been launched virtually complete, requiring only a further six-months for final fitting out. *(VT Group)*

The launch of the yacht ***Mirabella*** at Woolston in May 2003. Built for the American Entrepreneur Joe Vittorio at a cost of over £27m, she is the largest single masted yacht in the world, and the contract took VT into a new market on the back of their successful building of GRP and composite warships. ***Mirabella*** was delivered to her owner in May 2004. *(VT Group)*

The bow section of ***HMS Nottingham*** under repair by Fleet Support Ltd at Portsmouth on April 2nd 2003. The Woolston built ship ran aground on rocks off Lord Howe Island off Australia's east coast in July 2002 and the flooding was so severe that she was nearly lost. Only the superb damage control training and procedures saved the ship. She was transported back to the UK by heavy lift ship arriving at Portsmouth in December 2002. The ship commenced post refit trials in April 2004. *(VT Group)*

A close up of the bow section repairs to ***HMS Nottingham*** at Portsmouth in April 2003. The extensive structural work involved the replacement of over 120 tons of hull steelwork, and work to correct sea water corrosion. Over 12 miles of electrical cable was replaced along with the sonar, and considerable work was needed on the operational areas beneath the 4.5-inch gun and Sea Dart magazine. Both of the RR Olympus gas turbines were replaced. The ship was handed back to the RN in July 2004. *(VT Group)*

The pre-fabricated bulbous bow section is positioned on the building slip ready for welding to the main hull module of the River Class Offshore Vessel ***HMS Tyne*** in the main covered shipbuilding hangar at Woolston. The River Class were designed using a Computer Aided Design system and the large steel plates are manufactured using a Plasma cutting machine. The ship was built in large modules prior to assembly on the building berth. The opening for the bow thruster can be clearly seen in this photograph. *(VT Group)*

The third River Class OPV ***HMS Mersey*** rides high in the River Itchen just after launching at Woolston in 2003. The unique hull shape and bulbous bow can be clearly seen. The main hull has a very high freeboard to counter the rough sea conditions that the ship will operate in carrying out her main role of fishery protection. ***HMS Mersey*** has the unique distinction of being the last steel warship built by the Company at Woolston, and her completion marked the passing of an era for the city of Southampton. *(VT Group)*

Still flying the Red Ensign, the River Class OPV ***HMS Severn*** undergoes contractors sea trials in the Solent in the summer of 2003. The River class are leased to the RN under a 5 year agreement for which VT take responsibility for maintenance and support. At the end of the lease, the RN can either charter the ships, purchase them outright, or return them to VT. As part of the deal, VT has had to guarantee increased availability over the previous Island Class vessels to justify the replacement of five vessels by just three. *(VT Group)*

Nearly 70 years after she was built, the restored ***MTB 102*** sails through the gathered warships in the Solent, in June 2005, to take her place in the Trafalgar 200 International Fleet Review.
(Dave Cullen)

The new modular VT shipbuilding facility in Portsmouth Naval Base fronting onto C Lock was opened in the summer of 2003. Shipbuilding moved to Portsmouth as the Woolston Yard required substantial investment to update to modern shipbuilding methods and of course the River Itchen still limited the size of ship that could be launched. The new Portsmouth yard will first be used to fabricate modules for the new Type 45 Destroyers ordered for the RN, currently the largest ships to be constructed by the VT Group. The yard is also capable of building the mega-blocks envisaged for the construction of the RN's two new Aircraft Carriers. *(VT Group)*

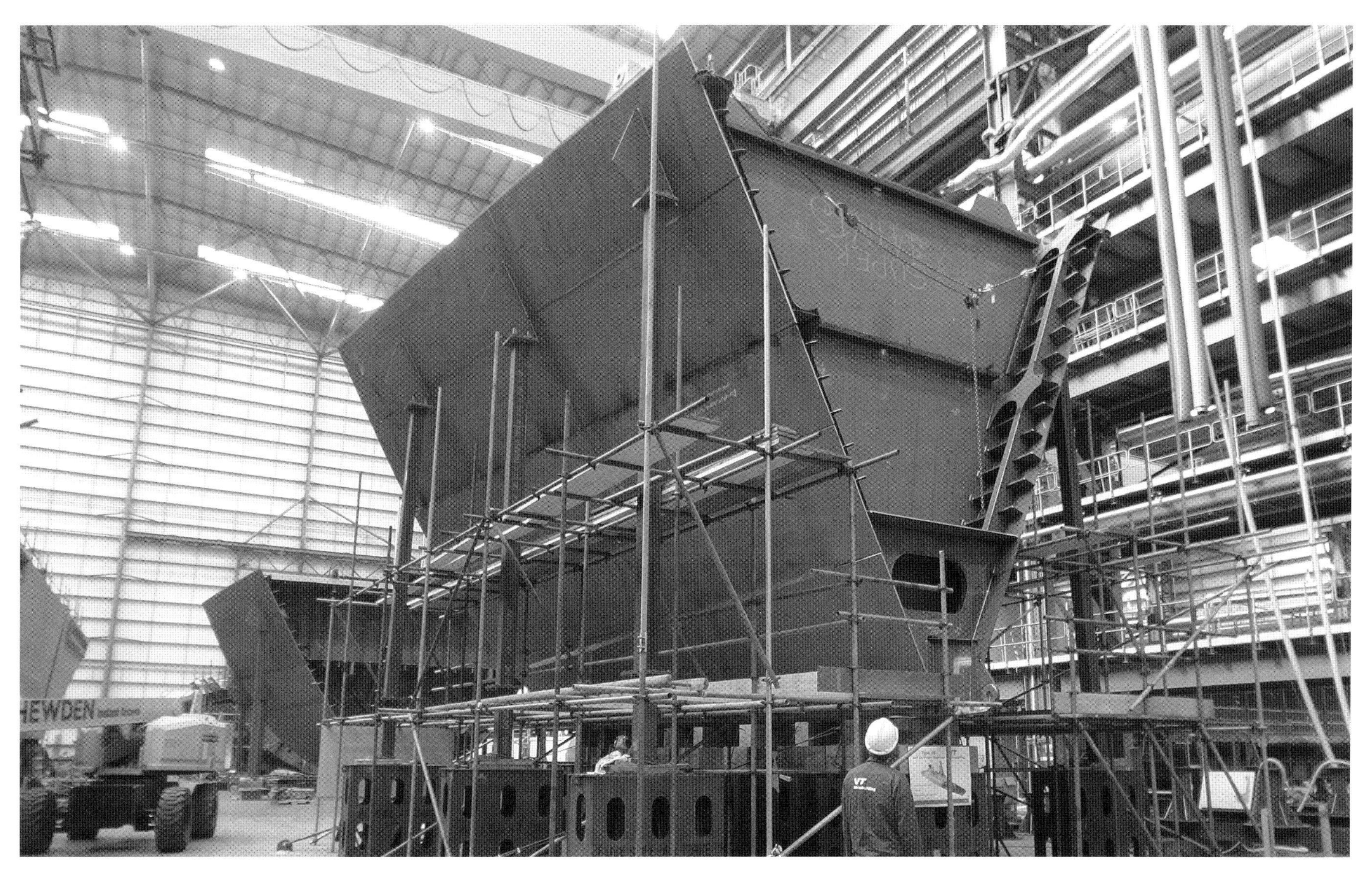

A bow section module for the first Type 45 Destroyer ***HMS Daring*** under assembly in the new £40m VT Group shipbuilding facility in Portsmouth Naval Base in May 2004. Shipbuilding moved from Woolston to Portsmouth in 2003 specifically to assemble the Type 45 Destroyer as the capacity of the Woolston yard to build the 7,000 ton ships was limited. *(VT Group)*

A view of the partly dismantled Woolston shipyard taken on 8 August 2004 from the Itchen bridge. The two GRP ship building hangars nearest Southampton Water have already been demolished and the crane that once lifted machinery and equipment into ships alongside the fitting out quay is now being used to demolish the main covered assembly building. The yard is rapidly being reduced to scrap for redevelopment into a shopping and housing complex. *(Author's Collection)*

The 1,200 ton completed bow section of the first Type 45 Destroyer, ***HMS Daring***, left the Portsmouth shipbuilding facility secured aboard the purpose built VT barge ***Woolston***, en route to the BAE Systems Scotstoun site on the Clyde in June 2005. The bow module is assembled upside down to allow ease and speed of welding, and is then rotated upright to allow final finishing and fitting out. At the time of the roll out, the shipbuilding facility had the first Type 45 bow sections under construction and were starting to cut metal on the new OPV(H), ***HMS Clyde***. *(VT Group)*

Construction of a new 80 metre patrol vessel was started in June 2005. The prefabricated stern section of the OPV(H) ***HMS Clyde*** is seen just after it was lowered onto the building berth in the ship building hall at Portsmouth Naval Base. The module was fabricated upside down for ease of welding, and rotated before being placed on the berth. The twin 'A' brackets for the propellors are clearly visible in this early 2006 view. The new design is based on the River class but is enhanced by the addition of a flight deck capable of accepting helicopters up to the size of the Merlin. ***HMS Clyde*** is to replace the Falkland Islands patrol vessels, ***Leeds Castle*** and ***Dumbarton Castle***.

(VT Group)

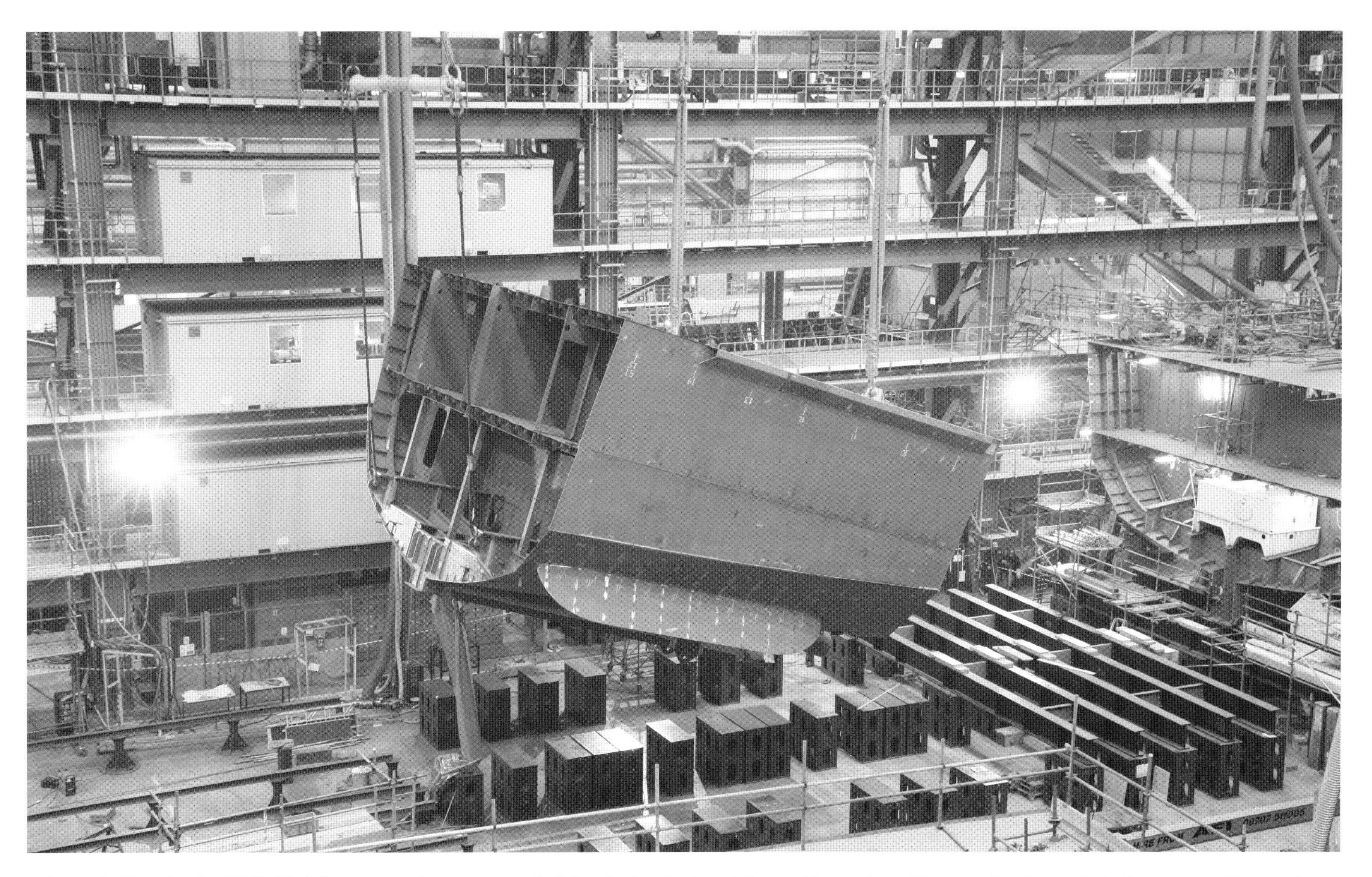

A further hull section for ***HMS Clyde*** is rotated and placed on the building berth. The large bilge keel is clearly visible as are the almost clinically clean conditions enjoyed at the facility. Similar to the earlier River class, the ship is owned by VT Group and chartered to the Ministry of Defence for a period of five years. At the end of that period, the MoD can either extend the charter, return the ship or purchase her outright. The new vessel will be available for 282 days a year. *(VT Group)*

The almost structurally complete hull of ***HMS Clyde*** in the ship building hall in the spring of 2006. The ship has yet to have her superstructure fitted but this has been constructed in an adjacent area within the hall, and would be lifted on, almost totally fitted out, within a few days. The ship is but a few weeks from the late June roll out date. *(VT Group)*

The first Type 45 Destroyer, ***HMS Daring***, is arrested by the drag chains as she enters the River Clyde after launching by the Countess of Wessex on 1 February 2006. VT Shipbuilding has played a key role in the design of the 7,350 ton ship and is contracted to build the bow sections, masts and funnels of the first six ships of the class under a sub contract to the main contractors, BAE Systems. The stealthy superstructure, to reduce the radar cross section of the ship, can be clearly seen. The Type 45 Destroyer is the first major warship in the Royal Navy to incorporate and integrated electric drive system for propulsion, weapons and hotel services. *(BAE Systems)*

The new OPV(H) ***HMS Clyde*** is rolled out of the Portsmouth ship building hall on 14 June 2006 and lowered from the wheeled launching trolleys onto the support jigs, on the barge VT Woolston, in preparation for the move into the adjacent dry-dock, from where she will be "launched." *(VT Group)*

HMS Clyde is moved into the dry-dock ready for the complex "launch" procedure. The dry dock was pumped dry after which the tie down welds were cut and the barge flooded. Once the water was pumped back into the dock, the ship was able to float free - the barge remaining on the bottom of the dock. The ship was due for completion and handover to the RN towards the end of 2006 and is due to deploy to the Falkland Islands in late March 2007. *(VT Group)*

Index

Abdiel 90
Albatross 11
Amazon (1908) 16
Amazon (1971) 103
Antelope 103,104,105
Artemiz 96

Barzan (1975) 106
Barzan (1995) 132
Bicester 126
Blackwood 77
Bluebird 65
Boat Shop 53
Boilers 29
Bold Pathfinder 72
Brave Borderer 79,81
Brecon (1942) 51
Brecon (1980) 109,115
Brissenden 54
Broad St Yard 70,71,91,116

Cable & Wireless 140
Clyde 156,157,158,160,161
Coastal MTB 17
Concord 69
Crossbow 64
Crusader 68
Cutlass 98
Cygnet 12

Daring (1893) 9
Daring (Type 45) 153,155,159
Dat Assawari 101
Defensora 104
Dhofar 116
Diesel Engine 13
Dorina 100
Duchess i,73
Dulverton 122

E33 20
E34 23
Essington 84

F3 22
Ferocity 78

Gay Bombadier 74
Gladfly 14
Gloucester 114,123,124,125
Glowworm 33
Grimsby 129
Gurkha 82,126

Hasanuddin 124,126
Hubberston 108
Hurworth 120,124,126
Hydraulic Press 31

Juno 92,94

Kalaat Beni Rached 124
Kashmir 42
Kromantse 89

Lance 18
Latona 47
Ledbury 115
Lightning 5

Machine Shop 28
Magpie 57
Mastiff 21
Mauretania 27
Melik 10
Mersey 149
Micheal 19
Mirabella 145
Mohawk 34
MTB T3 37,38
MTB 35 40
MTB 40ft 41
MTB 69 56
MTB 74 49
MTB 100 36
MTB 102 35,36,151
MTB 220 39
MTB 347 43
MTB 355 60
MTB 381 58
MTB 385 59
MTB 523 62
MTB 538 66
Muheet 134,136
Mussandam 131

Nautilus 4
Niteroi 102,104
Nottingham 111,112,119,120,146,147

Opportune 50
Otago 80

Packard Merlins 52,55
Peacock 61
Pembroke 135
Perkasa 93
Peru hulls 83
Popham 75
Portsmouth NB 152
Portchester Yard 67

Qatar 56m FAC 133,137
Qhair-Al-Amwaj 138,139

RAF 2564 44
RAF 2575 45
RAF 2576 46
RAF 2747 76
Ramadan 117,118

Saam 99
Sabre 98
Saguenay 32
Sandown Class 128
Sandown 130
Scimitar 98
Sea Wraith 141
Severn 150
Shakespeare 25
Shoreham 144
Sluys 96
Soloven 87,88
Southampton 107,110,111,112113,120,121
Speedy (1893) 7,8
Speedy (1918) 26

Tartar 15
TB 6 14
Teazer 24
Triton 143
Turbine Shop 30
Tyne 148

Umoja 127
Ursa 61

VSV Halmatic 142

Wilton 97
Woolston Quay 85,86,136,154

Zeltin 95
Zest 61